Next-Level Leadership

Juston C. Pate

First published by Dog Ear Publishing
4011 Vincennes Rd
Indianapolis, IN 46268
www.dogearpublishing.net

ISBN: 978-1-4575-4485-9

This book is printed on acid-free paper.

Printed in the United States of America

Table of Contents

Dedication

This book is dedicated to my wife, Jena, and our daughter, Caroline.

Introduction

Welcome to *Next-Level Leadership*. I'm glad we'll be spending some time together and I'll do everything I can to make it both valuable and enjoyable. My goal is to help you grow as a leader by providing opportunities to think about the profession and its fundamental skills. I just don't want to do it in a very technical or textbook fashion. All I want to do is share some stories and perspectives that will give you chances to think about leadership from a different point-of-view and perhaps use that viewpoint to help enhance your own skills.

Really, it's those perspectives and experiences we should seek when developing ourselves as leaders. Leadership lessons are all around us. We just have to be looking for them. I've learned just as much from watching others and reading biographies as I have from leadership classes or seminars. As long as we're looking for those lessons, we will find them. Sometimes in very unexpected ways.

I was sitting at work one day going through an endless list of emails, when I came across a note from my wife, Jena. We don't write each other using email very often, so it's always a nice surprise to see her name in my inbox. That is, until I saw the subject line. It read, "Marriage Isn't for You." Now, that's not what I was expecting to see. I was further troubled when I read her first line of text: *This reminds me of you.*

Needless to say, I was a little concerned. As it turned out, the email contained a link to a wonderful story about a young man who was struggling to come to grips with the thought of living a married life. More and more his fiancé was getting on his nerves, and the life he enjoyed seemed to be slipping away. He became increasingly nervous, and ultimately went to his father for guidance. He told his dad how he was feeling and asked if he should still get married. His father replied, "Son, I don't think marriage is for you."

The young man was shocked. He thought his dad would tell him that things would get better or that he might want to delay the wedding. He didn't expect to hear that marriage wasn't for him. Then his father went on to explain, "You see, you're being selfish. You don't marry to make yourself happy. You marry to make someone else happy. Marriage isn't supposed to be for you. Marriage is supposed to be for your wife. If you change your perspective, you will be just fine, son."

Now that's a powerful philosophy! You don't marry to make yourself happy. You marry to make someone else happy. Think of the bond that husbands and wives would build by adopting that point-of-view in their relationship.

It's a concept that extends beyond marriage, though. Anyone can build stronger bonds by adopting that attitude. In fact, it's the key to becoming a great leader. You don't lead to add value to your life. You lead to add value to everyone else's.

Leaders have to look at their responsibilities and interactions a little bit differently. Well, the successful ones do, anyway. The leadership point-of-view should be focused on the ones who are being led. When you take your leadership ability to the next level, you're really shifting your focus from making *yourself* better to making *everyone else* better. It's a lot like coaching. Coaches don't have to be the best players, they just have to prepare the players to be the best they can be.

Still, it takes a lot of work to be that type of leader. I believe in the John Maxwell principle known as the *Law of the Lid*, which basically states that the skill of the leader determines the potential of the team. In other words, the more skilled the leader, the more a team is capable of doing. That's why it's so important to improve your abilities. Leadership development isn't just about you. It's about enhancing the skills that will allow you to improve everyone else.

The catch is it takes a lot of time to develop those abilities. Becoming a leader doesn't happen overnight. If you earn a promotion or take a different job, you don't go to bed one night and wake up a leader the next morning.

Leadership is a drastically different job than whatever we were initially trained to do, and it requires new fundamental skills and a new way of thinking. It's just like the difference between any other two professions. For example, think of the following careers: psychology and plumbing. They are very different paths and require two completely different training programs. For people to excel in either, they would have to spend a great deal of time developing skills unique to that profession. Now, would you consider a psychologist a plumber, simply if she or he was hired as a plumber?

Of course not. So why is it different with leadership? Why would we consider a salesman a leader just because we made him a sales manager? Why would we consider a teacher a leader just because we made her a principal? Why would we consider a nurse a leader just because we made him a director? Well, we can't. That's where a lot of young leaders miss the boat, though. They think that by taking the position the lessons will come with experience. If you're not prepared to make the most of the experience, however, the lessons can be pretty overwhelming.

The good news is that any skill can be developed if you're willing to put in the effort, and leadership skills are no exception. Leaders should constantly strive for the next level. When people are promoted to mid-level management positions, they shift their focus from personal job duties to training, workloads, and resources. As they get closer to the "top," the focus changes again to policy, mission, outreach, and personnel. As assignments, roles, and responsibilities change and grow, so must you. Advancements in status must be accompanied with advancements in skill.

In a nutshell, *Next-Level Leadership* is not about you. It's about your effect. That's why your development matters. Leaders are ultimately responsible for making a positive contribution to the lives and work of others. Of course, to do that, you have to be good enough to make that positive contribution.

The tricky part about developing yourself as a leader is figuring out what parts to develop. There are many leadership styles and literally hundreds of leadership skills. At the most basic level, though, all successful leaders have three things in common: they choose the right direction, they align people's work with that direction, and they influence others to follow them.

This book is intended to highlight the fundamental skills that are most important to those three areas. Throughout these chapters we'll talk about the skills that relate to choosing the right direction (Integrity, Awareness, Philosophy, Planning, and Decision-Making), aligning work with goals (Alignment, Communication, Change-Leadership, Implementation, and Accountability), and building influence with others (Attitude, Trust, Relationships, Self-Confidence, and Influence).

We'll discuss many great leaders such as Dr. Martin Luther King, Jr., George Washington, John Wooden, Mahatma Gandhi, Mother Teresa, Pat Summitt, and many other great men and women. These leaders truly demonstrated a capacity for next-level leadership, and we can learn a great deal from their example. I will also share some insight and experiences from my own life so you can get a firsthand account of what has worked well and not so well for me. My hope is that these stories both inform and entertain as we work together to be all that we can be in this great profession.

So, I challenge you to make the most of the time we'll spend together and make some positive changes in your life as a leader. It's often been said that you can be anything you want to be in the world today, but I don't necessarily agree. We don't really live in a time when you can be anything you *want* to be. We live in a time when you can be anything you *work* to be. Leadership is no different. You can't be a great leader just by holding a great position. If you want to be a great leader, you can do it; you just have to be willing to put in the effort. If you do, you will lead your life in a more positive direction, but more importantly you will do the same for the people who choose to follow you.

Choosing Direction

Leadership without direction is more dangerous

than direction without leadership.

Next-Level Integrity

Wisdom is knowing the right path to take...
Integrity is taking it.

M. H. McKee

Any discussion of leadership or leadership ability should start with integrity. Nothing plays a more critical role in the way we shape ourselves, our profession, and our development. Sometimes we avoid that discussion, though, because it's hard to teach integrity. In fact, it's such a broad concept that it can be difficult to define.

Leadership integrity can be even harder to describe, since the integrity of the leader applies to the actions of a team. Experts such as Bernard Bass have defined leadership integrity as "the virtue of leaders who do what they say they will do, keep their promises, admit mistakes, and follow through on their commitments." I'd say that's a pretty good definition, but we could really boil it down to doing the right things for the right reasons. Those things and those reasons may not always be popular and they may not always be easy, but they are expected from the people we trust to choose our directions and futures.

When someone is trying to decide whether or not to follow you, it's not your ability to plan, make decisions, or communicate that matters most to them. It's your integrity. Don't believe me?

Then let me ask you this question: Would you follow Adolph Hitler? I'm willing to bet the answer is no. Even though Hitler's leadership skills allowed him to unify and mobilize an entire nation, we don't remember him based on the quality of his leadership. We remember him based on the quality of his integrity.

In matters of leadership, *you* matter. When you focus on your integrity you will develop your life, but more importantly you will develop a life others will want to follow. General Dwight D. Eisenhower believed, "In order to be a leader a (person) must have followers. And to have followers, a (person) must have their confidence. Hence the supreme quality for a leader is unquestionably integrity."

The great thing about integrity is that it just comes down to your choices. You don't have to possess a certain amount of talent, and it will never be a matter of physical ability. With elements such as communication, decision-making, awareness, change-leadership, and implementation, your circumstances and skills can have a significant impact on your results. With integrity, you are in control. Any leader can choose to act in the best interest of others, to uphold the mission of their organization, or to simply do the right things.

Of all the reasons integrity matters, it's most direct application is in the effect of the decisions we make. Those decisions set the standards for the work and behavior of all those who follow. When others are bound by your choices, you owe it to them to make the effects of those choices as positive as they can be. It's that effect that matters, and it's often shaped by your integrity. Although there are thousands of examples of the influence of integrity, one of the most powerful can be found in your own living room every evening.

Around 50 years ago, television networks could not show a man and a woman lying in bed together and foul language wasn't even considered. The moral standards were set very high, and anyone who watched a TV show could expect to see strong moral choices and personal conduct. Now, think about where we are today. Even the commercials for children's shows are more controversial than those standards. Over time, the bar has been lowered bit-by-bit. Network executives have made decisions to chase higher ratings by increasing the shock-value of their programs instead of protecting the integrity of their profession and their viewers. Today, whether you agree with it or not, we have to live with the choices made by those executives. If the leaders of the major networks had held to a higher standard, our airwaves wouldn't be filled with sex, drama, and violence.

It's the leader who makes the choices that affect the standards everyone else is expected to set for themselves. One leader who chose to adhere to a higher standard was Roy Vagelos. When Roy was the CEO of Merck Pharmaceutical Company, his scientists developed a drug to cure river blindness. It was a terrible disease that usually appeared in high poverty tribes and communities along river banks in third-world countries. The discovery had the potential to make a difference for thousands of people. Of course, the problem was that none of the people who needed the drug could pay for the treatment.

Roy tried to find donors or government grants to help market and distribute the drug, but had no luck. If Merck chose to distribute the treatment, the entire burden of the campaign would rest squarely on their shoulders. Vagelos knew what he wanted to do, but he was not just spending his money; he was spending the company's money.

Luckily, his beliefs firmly aligned with the philosophy of the Merck Corporation and its founders, who believed that medicine was for people, not profits. In just a few short years the drug was distributed to hundreds of thousands of people, preventing death and disease and restoring settlements in some of the most vibrant regions of Africa.

The decision to act with integrity didn't cost Merck, though. From that point on, the company was able to recruit the very best scientists who wanted to be a part of such an outstanding company. It was those scientists who went on to develop many profitable drugs and make Merck an industry leader. *The New York Times* wrote that Merck's contribution "will surely rank as one of the country's great medical triumphs." Vagelos simply called it the company's finest moment.

Next Level: Adding Value to Others

Integrity is much more than just a workplace principle. Organizations are not just a place to punch a time clock and do a job. Our places of employment are also sources of social contact, personal growth, community interaction, and moral development. If you want to truly add value to your teammates' lives, you can't focus all your energy on leading their work. You have to lead them. Just as children may not go to church or get up for school if their parents don't provide the structure and discipline, your employees may not build a life of integrity for themselves if you don't set the expectation and the example.

Anyone on the team has the potential to breach ethics and would also be subject to the consequences of his or her actions. If we truly care for and support our team members, we will not want them to face these situations. We don't just hold everyone to higher ethical standards to protect ourselves and our careers. We hold everyone to higher standards to protect them and their careers.

Next-level leaders are proactive rather than reactive when it comes to moral and ethical behavior. I would rather create opportunities to talk about cultural, team, and workplace expectations before situations occur rather than afterwards. You don't protect someone by telling them how to recover from bad choices. You protect them by teaching them to make good ones in the first place.

To do this, though, you have to stay in touch with your teammates and what they do. For example, one of President Ronald Reagan's greatest strengths was also his greatest weakness. He empowered his people to do their own work and trusted them to do it, but he often didn't follow up on what they were actually doing. During his eight years in office, there were over 100 incidents of illegal or immoral activities reported. Those problems didn't occur because of Reagan's integrity; they happened because he didn't ensure everyone else's.

Where We Go Wrong

We commit a breach of trust.

A breach of trust can negate years of hard work and solid performance in any relationship. This was a lesson Barry Bonds, Mark McGwire, and Sammy Sosa learned the hard way. Bonds, McGwire, and Sosa were three of the best baseball players in Major League Baseball history and excited a world of sports fans by breaking several homerun records during the 1990s. Unfortunately, all three fell from grace during the steroid scandal that followed. These men were well on their way to Hall of Fame careers without the benefit of any performance enhancing drugs. Their desire for more, however, led them to make unethical choices that ultimately led to a breach of trust.

For leaders, this is a terribly important concept. Every interaction or decision has the potential to strengthen or weaken your bond of trust with your teammates. Living by strict standards of integrity will do more to help you ensure that bond than anything you can do, and it makes it much easier for your teammates to choose to follow you. If people have to worry about whether or not you can be trusted, you won't have to worry about them following you very far.

We say one thing but do another.

"Do as I say, not as I do" does not apply to leadership. It's just a saying that allows people to avoid accountability for their actions. Mahatma Gandhi taught this lesson many years ago by adhering to the simple principle, "Your life is the message." You see, integrity may provide the meaning, but your life provides the message. You don't prove your integrity by what you say. You prove your integrity by what you do.

Many leaders are aware of the importance of their actions, so they try to act right. The problem is that they are only acting. Italian philosopher Niccolò Machiavelli even maintained in *The Prince* that leaders didn't actually have to be moral, they just had to appear moral. Believe me when I say, though, it's a much easier life when you don't have to pretend, conceal, or deceive when it comes to your ethics.

When people know you will do the right thing, regardless of the situation, it's much easier for them to follow your direction and your example. Management author James L. Hayes once wrote, "If people are careless about basic things – telling the truth, respecting moral codes, proper professional conduct – who can believe them on other issues?" When you behave honestly and expect others to do the same, the entire team feels better about being associated with you and where you're taking them.

We only apply integrity to personal values.

While our personal integrity is the foundation of who we are, leadership integrity applies to much more than just what we believe and how we feel. Doing the right things the right way will always lead you down the right path; we just have to understand that philosophy applies to all areas of our work. There are five basic types of integrity that apply to organizational and workplace interactions: foundational, work, interpersonal (or relational), team, and leadership. Each carries its own set of responsibilities, and each plays a role in fulfilling your obligation to act as a leader and a productive member of a team.

Foundational Integrity: Your foundational integrity is a collection of beliefs and values that are very important to you, personally. The catch? They may or may not be shared by other members of your team or organization.

Work Integrity: While we most often associate the values of integrity with our personal beliefs, the true nature of integrity is the effect it has on others. One of these effects is the work we do on a daily basis. Your work integrity will determine how you approach the quantity and quality of what you do while you're on the job. It includes aspects such as time management, preparation, skill, and all areas generally associated with a work ethic.

Interpersonal Integrity: While our effect on the organization is most closely linked to the job we were hired to do, the most direct impact of our integrity is on the people with whom we work. When you think about the reasons we want integrity in the workplace, the most important of all is that we have a positive effect on our teammates. After all, that's the whole point. Integrity isn't for us, it's for everyone else.

Team Integrity: As it truly relates to the relationships in any company or organization, though, integrity should apply to your ability to operate within a team. For any endeavor to be successful in a team environment, each individual has to be committed to the principles of unity and collaboration. Without that type of focus, no team can achieve at high levels.

Leadership Integrity: To me, though, there is no more important integrity than that of leadership. Leaders don't just *interact* with people's lives; they *impact* people's lives. Whether we talk about choosing direction, aligning work with goals, or building influence with others, the integrity of the leader affects the direction of the team.

We confuse healthy aspiration with toxic ambition.

There is nothing wrong with a healthy aspiration for achievement. It's one of the greatest motivators of performance I have ever seen. In fact, research has shown that it's one of the strongest predictors of success. With that type of attitude, no one has to push you to achieve your goals; you push yourself.

Aspiration can be dangerous, however, if it becomes a toxic ambition. Ambitious people may be high achievers, but they are also highly competitive. A competitive nature is often the pathway to getting any "edge" one can get. That's where we can get in trouble with our ethics. Achievement and success don't come easy. The shortcuts are often really tempting, especially if they can save us time or make us money. That's why integrity matters. When faced with immoral opportunities to advance, it's those with a strong foundation who will continue to do the right thing.

How to Uphold Integrity

Develop a strong code of ethics.

Sometimes people fail ethically because they are just unethical people. They are aware of right and wrong, but choose to do wrong. Other times, however, people fail ethically because they underestimate the power of temptation. Temptation is a strong force, and one that is all around you. Each day any one of us could be tempted to lie, cheat, or spread gossip about a neighbor. Whether it's something large or something small, the best way to deal with temptation is to become so grounded in what you believe to be right that you don't even consider any actions you believe to be wrong.

Warren Buffet has always been fond of saying, "You look for three qualities in people: integrity, intelligence, and energy. And if they don't have the first, the other two will kill you." Ability can take you a long way in life, but only if you have the principles to guide you in the right direction. A personal code of ethics allows you to make choices based on a set of predetermined rules rather than circumstances or passing notions.

Many people believe you have to develop a very detailed code of ethics to guide your life, but I think it should be just the opposite. The simpler the code the more likely you will remember it during the difficult times. Personally, I try to live my life by four simple guiding principles:

1. I want to live by Christian values.
2. I want my wife to respect me and what I do.
3. I want my daughter to say, "That's my dad, and I'm very proud of him."
4. I want to act in the best interest of my teammates.

It's a simple little code, but it certainly guides the decisions I make.

Set high expectations.

If you truly want to avoid the little "gray areas" of ethics and integrity, set high expectations for your and your team's decisions and behaviors. Many times companies get themselves into trouble because they operate on the edge of morality in order to make a deadline, make a deal, or make an extra dollar. The trouble is, when the standards are low, it's just a short drop to unethical behavior.

When you set the standards of integrity very high, you don't have to worry quite as much about the gray areas. It's a lot easier to help someone recover from falling just short of meeting high standards of ethical performance than it is to help them recover from falling just short of low standards. Fall short of high standards and you may have to make an apology. Fall short of low standards and you may have to make bail.

Let other people help.

Once you have a solid foundation in place, you can ensure your ethical strength by instituting a system of safeguards. Any system of checks-and-balances should be embraced. For example, many managers despise audits, feedback, and transparency, but they are actually nothing more than means to ensure integrity. When you set highly transparent practices and give people the opportunity to offer feedback, it removes the temptation to bend the rules or hide the truth. When you know up front that everyone will know what you do, it's easier to keep yourself on the straight and narrow.

Personally, my greatest safety net in matters of integrity is the people I can count on to tell me like it is. I have been fortunate to have some very strong people in my life who have done just that. From my wife to my coworkers, I have no shortage of people who will tell me when they think I'm about to go down the wrong path. I may not always like what they have to say, but because they say it, I've had a much easier time distinguishing right from wrong. When you have no one in your life from whom you can receive honest feedback regarding ethical matters, you'll find the line between right and wrong isn't nearly as easy to define.

Use the ethical guides around you.

We all have moral guides we can use to help keep us on the right path. Standards such as *The Ten Commandments* or *The Golden Rule* set parameters within which we can base our behaviors. For example, one of the best measures I have found in my life and career by which to make ethical business decisions is the *Four-Way Test* used by Rotary International.

The *Four-Way Test* was first developed by Herbert Taylor in 1932 when he was hired as the president of the Club Aluminum Products Company. Club Aluminum had been losing money and was in danger of closing their doors. Taylor knew that to have any hope of saving the troubled company he had to first put them on a path of moral strength. He wanted to use a simple but thorough measure by which all employees, from top to bottom, could make ethical choices. To do this he instituted the following four questions all employees had to ask themselves before taking any action:

The Four Way Test

Is it the truth?

Is it fair to all concerned?

Will it build goodwill and better friendships?

Will it be beneficial to all concerned?

Eleven years later, Rotary International adopted the *Four-Way Test* and it has been repeated millions of times by thousands of Rotarians to help ensure a focus on integrity.

If you can't find an existing code by which you would like to live your life, you can still use a simple measure to help you make better decisions. It's called the newspaper test. When facing a decision about ethics, just ask yourself, "How would it look if my choice was printed on the front page of the newspaper?" If you wouldn't want the world to read about the decision you made, you probably shouldn't make that choice.

Basically, Next-Level Integrity Is...

...your foundation.

I firmly believe that great people are not great because of what they have accomplished on the outside. Great people are great because of who they are on the inside. Your integrity lays that foundation. It's the platform from which you build success, whether personal or professional. More importantly, it will allow you to sustain that success. Success isn't meant to be a moment. It's meant to be a lifestyle.

I was listening to a preacher one morning on the radio who was speaking on that very subject. He was talking about the importance of aligning your character and your skills. He said those who developed skills before they developed their character were setting themselves up to go somewhere their integrity wouldn't let them stay. When your focus is only on your ability you may find moments of success, but if that success is built on a faulty foundation, it may be stripped away just as quickly.

Unfortunately, the world has been filled with examples of people who built something their integrity wouldn't let them keep. Bernie Madoff was such an example. I don't think anyone could argue that Madoff was a successful investor. He took a $5,000 start-up fund and turned it into a multi-billion dollar corporation. His problem was that his personal foundation was not strong enough to keep him from being driven by ambition and greed. He began crossing ethical lines by using new investors' money to pay old investors' dividends and stealing millions from his clients. He found ways of making money faster by ignoring his integrity, but those actions ultimately cost him everything he had earned. Of course, it also cost the thousands of people who invested with him.

As a leader, your integrity affects more than your personal life. Its effect on your team and organization is just as important. Sometimes a lapse in personal integrity can lead to a loss of organizational integrity. That lapse can cost a good deal of money, such as the Enron scandal, but sometimes the consequences can be much more serious.

Consider the *Challenger* space shuttle disaster of 1986, for example. NASA contracted with Morton-Thiokol for several components of their space shuttles, including some of the O-ring gaskets that contained the pressurized fuels in the huge aircraft. In the days before the launch, the engineers at Morton-Thiokol discovered a potential problem with a critical O-ring in the booster rockets. Many of those engineers, especially Roger Boisjoly, believed the gasket would fail. Because of this, Morton-Thiokol strongly encouraged NASA to delay the launch.

When NASA balked at the suggestion and threatened to drop the contract if the O-rings were ineffective, the leaders at Morton-Thiokol decided to retract their initial recommendation so they wouldn't lose future business with NASA. Because of their lapse in integrity, the seven-member crew of the *Challenger* lost their lives when the O-ring burst and the fuel cells exploded. Had those leaders developed a stronger foundation for their company, they would have been more concerned with doing the right thing than their profit margin and the disaster could have been avoided.

I'll close this chapter with a piece called *The Paradoxical Commandments*, written by Kent Keith in 1968 as a college writing project. His words were later transcribed by Mother Teresa and hung on the wall of her Home for Children in Calcutta, India. When it comes to laying a foundation for a personal or corporate code of ethics, I'm not sure we could find a better guide.

The Paradoxical Commandments

People are illogical, unreasonable, and self-centered.
Love them anyway.

The good you do today will be forgotten tomorrow.
Do good anyway.

Honesty and frankness make you vulnerable.
Be honest and frank anyway.

Give the world the best you have and you'll get kicked in the teeth.
Give the world the best you have anyway.

Next-Level Awareness

The thing we desperately need is to face the way it is.

Theresa Mancuso

The choices we make regarding our directions and day-to-day decisions set the stage for everything we will accomplish in life. However, those decisions will only be as good as what we have done to prepare ourselves to make them. That preparation begins with an awareness of ourselves and our situations, and as leaders extends to others and their situations.

Leadership is not about you; it's about the effect you have on the people who follow you. That's the first and greatest responsibility of the leader, and it's why you should always make gaining awareness a top priority. There's so much to learn about all of the variables that affect your team and their direction. Since leaders make the decisions that have the most direct impact on our teammates, we owe it to them to learn all we can about those variables.

Of all the chapters in this book, this has been the most difficult to write. There are just so many aspects of people, places, and things about which leaders must be aware. Awareness helps you put people in the right position, provide proper support, align team goals with the environment, and align everyone's work with those goals. As complicated as it can be, though, leadership awareness really comes down to your understanding of yourself, your team, and your situation.

Awareness of Self

Self-awareness is a very important concept. Without it, no individual can be as good as he or she could possibly be. If we want more for ourselves and recognize that we need to make some type of improvement in order to get there, it means there is potential for growth. The trick is we have to know the difference between what we do and what we need to do.

James Clawson, of the Darden Graduate School of Business Administration, calls this the gap between the Ideal Self and the Actual Self. What he means is the difference between who we want to be and who we think we are. The hard part is recognizing that difference. Most folks have a pretty clear picture of who they want to be, but they don't have such an honest understanding of who they really are. Without that piece of the puzzle, though, you can't work to make changes to your current behaviors in order to get the most out of your life. As John Maxwell is fond of saying, "You have to know yourself before you can grow yourself."

Awareness of Others

Still, to make a positive contribution to the lives of others, you need to know a great deal about them, what they do, and what they are capable of doing. You never want to put someone in a position where their strengths are overshadowed by their weaknesses. People have varying skills, goals, and desires and are motivated in thousands of different ways. If you don't know your teammates well enough to know what motivates them and what they do, you will most likely default to leading them based on your preferences and experience. Of course, that may not work at all for them.

With an awareness of others comes the ability to know what needs to be done for their best interests. Without it, you can't lead your people because you won't know them or their circumstances. President Herbert Hoover experienced that lack of awareness during the Great Depression. He once famously said, "No one has starved, yet," when people were, in fact, starving. American citizens were getting themselves arrested just so they could eat. Hoover thought that the Great Depression was not affecting many people so he made his decisions regarding government support based on that understanding. He believed the government shouldn't extend itself to relieve individual suffering, but if he had known the severity of the suffering, he may have felt differently.

Leaders must understand the needs of their teammates in order to make the best decisions for them. President Hoover's choice to continually withhold Federal support was affected by his perspective. It had nothing to do with his willingness to help. That's why leaders can't look at the world based solely on their point-of-view. We don't make decisions for ourselves. We make decisions for everyone, and must take what I call the Leadership Point-of-View.

Taking the Leadership Point-of-View means that we must look at the world through the eyes of others. People's situations and experiences give them different understandings; therefore, you can't expect everyone to understand the world as you do. If you know enough about your teammates to know what they do and what they need, you stand a much better chance of connecting with them and making the best choices to help them.

Awareness of Situation

Great leaders gain awareness so they can navigate the future. The decisions you make today lay the foundation for tomorrow. For that foundation to be solid, those decisions have to be based on a strong awareness of your situation. Without that level of understanding, your choices and plans may not work because they may not align your actions with your circumstances.

There's an old success formula commonly used in business called the SAR Model. It stands for Situation, Action, Result. What it means is that for any situation, the actions you choose determine your results. Choose the right actions, and you'll get the best results. Of course, your awareness of the situation will determine what actions you choose.

General Mathew Broderick, who oversaw Homeland Security during the Bush administration, was charged with overseeing the levees in New Orleans during the 2005 Hurricane Katrina disaster. Despite multiple reports of breaches, Broderick ignored the data and left work on Monday, August 29th reporting that the levees were fine. Of course, they were not fine and a great tragedy followed. His lack of awareness about his situation led him to take the wrong action, and the results cost many lives and millions of dollars.

I always think of General George Custer and his "Last Stand" when discussing the importance of having an awareness of situation. Most people think that Custer's major downfall was his ego and his stubborn belief that he couldn't be defeated. That wasn't it, though. It was his lack of awareness. You see, his information about the Indian village he planned to attack was two to three weeks old.

Those reports estimated the total population of the village to be around three thousand, with only 800 warriors.

Custer had no doubt that his 480 well-armed men were more than capable of wiping out a village of that size. The problem was that his information wasn't up to date. The situation had changed, but his awareness hadn't. Since his last intelligence report, the village had gained over 3,000 inhabitants and the number of warriors grew to 2,000. I'd say that would have been a useful bit of information!

While most of us in the civilian world will never be placed in a position to make life-and-death decisions based on the quality of our information, we do face many challenging and changing situations that make it necessary for us to maintain a keen sense of awareness. Our teams expect that we will lead them in the right direction regardless of the current circumstances. As long as we understand those circumstances, we can do just that. The minute we lose sight of them, however, we may be leading everyone onto thin ice without even realizing it.

Next Level: Your Team's Awareness

Awareness is the first step toward adding value to your life and the lives of all those who follow you. With no awareness of your environment, you can't set your goals; without an awareness of your goals, you can't have a purpose; and without a purpose, you will never engage in meaningful work. You just have to realize that the same holds true for your teammates.

As businessman and leadership author Max Dupree once said, "The first responsibility of a leader is to define reality." The most important thing to realize is that reality won't be defined by what you know. It will be defined by what everyone else knows. Your awareness of self, others, and situation will give you the potential to set the right directions, but everyone else's awareness of self, others, and situation will make those directions work.

It's the job of the leader to make sure people have those types of awareness. To be aware of themselves, people have to know the truth about their performance. They need to know when they do something well so they will do it again, but they also must know when they do something wrong so they will not repeat the mistake. It's not easy to correct our teammates, and a lot of leaders choose to avoid that responsibility for fear of losing the relationship. That kind of thinking is bad enough in social relationships, but it's completely unacceptable in leader/follower relationships. The only thing worse than telling someone the truth about poor performance and losing them is withholding the truth about poor performance and keeping them.

Helping your teammates gain a solid awareness of themselves is critical, but the strongest teams have a solid awareness of what everyone else is doing, as well. People can't work within silos and be a part of a team. They may do good work that way but they will do so as individuals, not as teammates. The best teams are full of people who value one another. When everyone understands what others are doing and why they're doing it, it's much easier. It's hard to value what you don't understand.

Of course, none of this matters if your teammates don't have a solid understanding of their situation. The team must be clearly aware of their goals and their plans so they know exactly how to contribute. When leaders establish this awareness, they provide a platform for strong performance. Without that understanding, the team wastes time doing the wrong work or tries to figure out where to start. If you expect people to engage in meaningful work and find a purpose and passion for what they do, they have to be aware of where they're going, what they're doing, and why it matters.

In the end, the more your teammates know, the better your team will be. I've found in my career that when everyone has a very clear understanding of what's going on, they are able to make more valuable contributions to our plans and decisions. That, as much as anything else, has helped me get to the next level as a leader. You see, I've had a lot of good ideas over the years but I've had very few great ones. The only way I've been able to get from good to great is to raise the awareness of others and let them help.

Where We Go Wrong

We accept the story we want to hear.

Jack Welch, former CEO of General Electric, always advised his leaders, "Face reality as it is, not as it was, or as you wish it were." Every successful leader with whom I've ever worked has stuck to that philosophy. Too many leaders accept the good news but deny the bad news. That's a recipe for disaster. In fact, it's the recipe that sank the Titanic. Here's a paraphrased rundown of the conversation between the captain, his first mate, and his navigator:

Captain: How are we doing, men?

First Mate: Making good progress, sir. We're even a little ahead of schedule.

Captain: Great! We'll get to New York sooner than projected. We'll be heroes in every newspaper around the world!

First Mate: Yes, sir. As long as we don't have to change course we'll be fine.

Navigator: Excuse me sir, but I think we should change course to avoid some potential icebergs.

Captain: Are you sure we're going to hit them?

Navigator: No, sir, but I have data to show that we'll sink if we hit an iceberg, and I have data to show that we're heading for icebergs.

Captain: If we change course, will we still beat the projected time?

First Mate: No, sir. We'll miss it by about two hours.

Captain: Then I don't believe we'll hit the icebergs and we'll stay with the current course!

Awareness isn't gained by selectively hearing what we want to hear. It's gained by objectively hearing what is being said. It's not easy to do that, though. To gain objective awareness we have to be willing to hear a lot of hard truths in order to get a full understanding of our situation. You will succeed or fail based on how well you understand what is truly happening within your team and your environment. It's that kind of truth that will provide you with a proper perspective so that your understanding is based on reality. Avoiding hard truths doesn't alter that reality. It puts you at odds with it.

We gain self-awareness based on our point-of-view.

Gaining a true sense of self-awareness is difficult, but important to your effectiveness as a leader. Just realize that you will need help to get it. People will make the choice to follow you based on who <u>they</u> think you are, not who <u>you</u> think you are. When your image of yourself doesn't align with everyone else's image of you, it becomes very difficult to lead.

That type of misalignment means leaders and followers have a hard time connecting because the followers are not receiving what the leader thinks he or she is giving. For instance, I've known a lot of people who thought they were funny, so they kept telling jokes. Since they weren't funny, they just became annoying. Likewise, I've known a lot of managers who thought they were respected, so they acted like they were the boss. Since they weren't respected, they weren't effective.

To paraphrase poet Robert Burns, I wish the gift that God would give us was to see ourselves as others see us. Many leaders fail because they don't look at themselves through the eyes of others. You need to make sure that your self-image aligns with the image you project. If it doesn't, you'll struggle to gain respect and could lose your ability to unify your team. Whether it's something informal like honest conversations regarding your performance on a project or something more structured such as peer or subordinate evaluations, any efforts to collect feedback from your teammates will only serve to strengthen your ability to do your job. If you only assess what you think about yourself, you're missing the point. It's what others think about you that determines how far they will follow you.

We jump to inaccurate conclusions.

One of the deadliest social diseases of our time is conclusion jumping. It's bad enough when someone creates a false reality that affects their own world, but it's ten times worse when a leader creates a false reality that affects everyone else's. I've seen too many people cause harm by considering an assumption to be a fact until someone proves otherwise. Leaders have to train themselves to do just the opposite and consider nothing to be true until they have proof that it is.

Many times we jump to conclusions because we wait until it's too late to do anything else. To keep from this, we have to make every effort to gain awareness each and every day. You can't wait until a decision is necessary to try to learn about your teammates and your circumstances. Leaders who make awareness a priority every day are much more likely to ground their actions and decisions in reality. Those who wait until a critical moment to gain awareness may have to jump to a conclusion that takes them over the edge.

How To Gain More Awareness

Don't wait on awareness. Pursue it!

We all have blind spots, so to speak, where we don't know what is going on. In other words, we are ignorant of some aspect of reality. It's often been said that ignorance is bliss, but for leaders, ignorance is dangerous. To do your job well, you can't sit back and wait on awareness; you have to seek it. If you only rely on the information that comes on its own you'll be missing about 90% of what is really happening.

The good news is that awareness is all around you. As a leader you will have many resources available to help build your understanding, but the most important resource is your teammates. Your teammates have a wealth of knowledge and experience you can access just by asking a few questions. Most people are willing to share what they know. It's just up to you to initiate the conversation.

The key to making the most of your questions is to make sure people feel comfortable giving you honest answers. Your best bet is to surround yourself with great people and let them tell you what they think. You do this by supporting those who tell the truth, not punishing them. Punishing someone for giving an honest opinion doesn't change their opinion; it changes their honesty.

Spend time with your teammates.

We have to be with our team to gain their perspective, which is the perspective that really matters. This type of awareness is the cure for a disease I like to call Administrative Amnesia. Leaders often come down with Administrative Amnesia by losing their connection with the work and the workers. When that happens, their awareness rarely extends beyond an office or a boardroom. Decisions made about products and processes simply can't be effective if they are made without knowing what the people closest to the work are doing.

You can't make decisions without having insight, and you can't have insight without being in sight of your team. As bestselling author Wess Roberts wrote, "It is unfortunate when final decisions are made by chieftains headquartered miles away from the front, where they can only guess at conditions and potentialities known only to the captain on the battlefield."

People need to know that their leader understands them and their situation. In the days after the September 11th attacks on the World Trade Center Buildings in New York, Mayor Rudy Giuliani was with his people. He did not lead from the back. He did not run. He did not hide. He experienced what they were experiencing. He wanted to make well-informed and immediate decisions, and he knew he couldn't do that if he was removed from the situation. As a result, everyone knew their leader was acting in their best interests. For this, more than any other reason, he won the love and respect of his city and an entire nation.

Work on your emotional maturity.

It's not easy to gain awareness, and it's even harder to do so by seeing the world through the eyes of others. To grow as leaders, though, that's exactly what we have to do, and we must have a strong sense of maturity to do it. It's not easy to accept hard truths about ourselves, but when we are willing to consider them and what we need to improve, we give ourselves a much better chance to be all we can be. In fact, it's that type of maturity that sets our potential, not our current skill or our level of intelligence.

I think we place too much value in our society on IQ, or Intelligence Quotient. For leaders and those working in a team environment, a much better predictor of success is what Daniel Goleman calls EQ, or Emotional Quotient. EQ is a measure of your awareness regarding your own emotions and their effect. It's a quality that comes with maturity. People don't always recognize the value of emotional maturity because they see their careers as being connected to professions, jobs, or businesses. As leaders, our careers are connected to people. Our ability to control our emotions will often determine the strength of those connections.

Emotional maturity makes it possible to lead your teammates because it makes it possible for you to relate to them. Looking at things from your teammates' point-of-view means that you will be much less likely to assume the worst about their intentions. Author Matthew Reed once wrote, "One of my key strategies is to assume good faith, no matter how bizarre the initial assertion. Because no matter how weird their statements may sound, even people who are well off the mark generally think they're right. Until you figure out how they got there, you won't be able to reach them." It's really the first step of any effort to lead. You have to go where people are to know how to get them where they need to be. If you won't go where they are because you don't like where they're coming from, you'll more than likely just leave them behind.

In a Nutshell, Next-Level Awareness Is...

...experience.

Of course, I mean experience, not years-of-service. There's a big, big difference. Doing a job for a long time doesn't necessarily mean you've been learning from a job for a long time. I've known many teachers who say they've had thirty years of experience, when nothing could be further from the truth. What they've really had was one year of experience thirty times because they just kept doing the same things over and over. To truly gain experience, you can't just gain awareness. You have to make the most of your awareness by reflecting on the lessons you learn and changing how you behave as a result.

Just keep in mind that experience is gained so that you can do your job better. It's not gained just to know more. It's gained so you can <u>do</u> more. Experience is more than knowledge; it's the ability to draw on knowledge and make some kind of difference as a result. When you *have* an experience it becomes part of your past, but when you *gain* experience it changes who you are and what you can do in the future. It's basically the difference between being Knowledgeable and Knowledge Able. When you are Knowledgeable you have information, but when you are Knowledge Able you have the ability to take that information and do something with it.

<u>Knowledgeable People</u>	<u>Knowledge Able People</u>
Know Content	Use Content
Memorize	Learn
Cherish Information	Cherish Understanding
Ask questions that lead to more knowledge	Asks questions that lead to more possibilities
Know procedures	Know how to proceed
Hear information	Hear people

We don't gain awareness to know the right things. We gain awareness to do the right things. When you are Knowledgeable you have the potential to make a difference. When you are Knowledge Able you are likely to actually do it.

Next-Level Philosophy

Leaders without a philosophy are like a leaf not tied to the branch — they get blown anywhere the winds take them.

Murray Johannsen

I have never met a successful person who couldn't tell me why he or she was successful. Those people have all made very specific, intentional steps toward the accomplishment of their goals. They have had a detailed plan for their life, but more importantly they have had a personal set of rules or guiding principles to help them stick to that plan. It's those rules, not the plan, that made the difference for them.

Those guiding principles are called your philosophy, and it's very important. You see, anyone can have a goal, and anyone can set a plan to achieve that goal. The successful people make sure their daily decisions and behaviors align with that plan. It's the only way to ensure that the direction you choose (your potential) leads to where you want to be (your achievements). Philosophy is the bridge between potential and achievement. When your philosophy is strong enough to consistently align your behaviors with your plans, you will be in a better position to achieve your goals.

We hear the terms willpower and self-control more than we do philosophy, but they are all very similar. You see, when we think of people who demonstrate a strong willpower or a great deal of self-control, we think of people who can face temptation and stay true to what they believe or what they want to accomplish. Take two people who decide to quit smoking, for instance. One of them could stand in the middle of a smoky bar and never touch a cigarette. The other may have a slightly bad day at work and stop at the nearest gas station to pick up a pack. The difference between the two is what they've done to mentally prepare themselves to accomplish their goal. The person who chose not to smoke committed to that choice long before entering the bar.

The quality of your life is based on the quality of your choices, and your foundational philosophy determines those choices. It's why lottery winners or professional athletes can come into huge sums of money one year and find themselves completely broke the next. They had no set of guiding principles to frame the decisions they made about their spending, and ultimately lost control. If they had a stronger foundation from which to make better choices, they could have maintained their wealth. In other words, if their philosophy had been strong enough to guide their choices in a positive direction, they would have made the most of their good fortune.

The people who make the most significant contributions to the world are men and women of substance, not circumstance or strategy. Circumstances and strategies change too frequently to determine long-term success. Many people struggle to get ahead in life because they think their situation has to change in order for them to reach their goals. High achievers don't think that way, and that's why philosophy matters. Its purpose is to change your behavior, and a change in behavior will have a much greater impact on your circumstances than a change of circumstances will have on your behavior.

The catch is people don't change their behavior. They change their focus. They change their mindset. They change their values. In other words, they change their thinking. Your thoughts determine the choices you make, which ultimately determine your behaviors. If you want to change the way you act, you have to change the way you think. Philosophy provides structure for your thoughts, which ultimately provides structure for your actions.

The most important aspect of philosophy is that it allows us to focus on the most important behaviors by making them a priority in our thoughts, and in that way making those behaviors habitual. As it applies to leadership, when you develop a strong philosophy based on successful fundamentals and values, you will be much more likely to develop positive leadership habits. Leaders who develop good habits will be much more likely to achieve their goals and add value to the lives of others. Leaders who develop bad habits will struggle to succeed because their behaviors will serve as a continual barrier.

To be honest, I never really thought there'd be a time in my life when I would value philosophy. I always thought of myself as more of a doer than a thinker, so I just didn't think it would be important to my life. Philosophy seemed to be something for people who thought a lot and talked a lot, but didn't do a lot. What I have come to realize is that without the structure of a guiding philosophy, the things I do don't necessarily lead to the things I want. Since my greatest desire is to add value to the lives of my teammates, there's too much riding on my actions to leave them up to chance.

Next Level: Setting Clear Expectations

Your philosophy is your guide for the choices you will make, but as the leader that philosophy also provides the values your team will be likely to adopt as their own. Your philosophy will let people know what to expect from you and what you expect from them. I once had the chance to visit with U. S. Army Lt. Colonel Fred Bates, who told me, "Our philosophy is what establishes the boundaries of what is acceptable. If we keep our behaviors inside those boundaries we'll be successful. It's when we stray outside those lines that we get into trouble."

Having this type of guide makes it much easier to make good decisions. The "boundaries" Lt. Colonel Bates mentioned help everyone maintain a positive direction. Decisive teams have clearly established those guidelines. Indecisive teams have to wonder about them. If everyone has a clear understanding of what is acceptable and what is not, they don't have to spend time and energy wondering what to do. They can be confident and decisive while they keep moving forward.

The key is to keep your philosophy simple and understandable. It should be easy for people to know the difference between right and wrong. If you want your teammates to adopt your philosophy as a guide for their own behaviors, the first step is to help them understand it. When philosophies are complex or complicated, it gets harder to understand where the lines are drawn. For example, Hall-of-Fame coach Lou Holtz had three basic rules for his football teams:

1. Do what's right and avoid what's wrong.

2. Do whatever you do to the best of your ability.

3. Show people that you genuinely care.

He found he didn't need anything more complicated than that to establish the boundaries for acceptable and unacceptable behavior on his teams.

Many of the most successful companies in the world have followed similar patterns by creating some type of easy-to-understand philosophical standard. Starbucks put their philosophy in the *Green Apron Book* they distribute to every new employee. Basically, it outlines the five key values the leadership team considers to be most important. They are: be welcoming, be genuine, be knowledgeable, be considerate, and be involved. The *Green Apron Book* only takes about five minutes to read, but it provides clear boundaries for the employees' choices and behaviors. If it were 125 pages long and contained the 72 "most important" things, it would not be nearly as effective.

All-in-all, philosophy is intended to help us do what is right and what will guide us in the most positive direction. It's important to extend that guide to the rest of your team. You see, it's not enough to choose the right directions. The responsibility of leadership is greater than that. We are expected to do more than just choose our teammates' destination; we are expected to help them reach it. Goal-setting and planning may provide a path for success, but outlining a clear philosophy for decisions and behavior helps people keep from getting lost along the way.

Where We Go Wrong

We leave success up to chance.

There's an old proverb that reads, "He who trusts all things to chance, makes a lottery of his life." Personally, I have no desire to make a lottery of my life. The odds of winning are way too low. I'd rather up my odds by taking control of my decisions and behaviors, so I would rather build a strong philosophy to guide what I do.

Without a clear set of guiding principles to serve as an anchoring point for your behavior external forces are much more likely to control what you do. When you craft a philosophy, though, you're taking a great deal of chance out of your future. You are defining the skills and values you believe to be critical to success and working to make those behaviors automatic. Otherwise, you're just hoping that what you do will lead to success, and while hope is a great feeling, it's a pitiful plan.

Our values don't drive consistent behaviors.

Leaders who haven't made conscious decisions to define the values that will shape their leadership style often move back and forth between conflicting styles. Some days, those leaders may be strict disciplinarians. Other days, they may be lax and tolerant of missed deadlines. One week the leader may take time to get to know employees and spend time developing relationships, and the next week he or she may speak harshly to anyone who crosses their path. These types of swings confuse and frustrate employees, and they certainly do nothing to create a healthy work environment.

In order to build influence with your team, you will have to consistently take care of business and take care of them before they will believe in you. A strong philosophy is the key to that consistency. It becomes the default setting for your actions and interactions with others. Without it, your behaviors will be more strongly influenced by outside circumstances, and those change every day. If your teammates never know when you're going to be out of control or which direction you will choose, why would they feel like you will consistently make things better for them? Followers want to know their leaders have the discipline it takes to be counted on every day, not just every now and then.

We include too many "most important" things.

You have to be able to focus on the elements in your philosophy before they can make a difference in your behavior – and you can't focus on everything. When I first started playing golf, an elderly gentleman decided to give me some advice after watching me hit a few balls on the driving range. He walked over to me, put his hand on my shoulder, and said, "Son, you've got a fine natural swing, but you're missing a couple of fundamentals. You just need to think about keeping your head down a bit more, locking your left arm, pushing through with your right hand, keeping your chest on one plane, turning your hips completely through the ball, finishing higher on your swing, ending with the club a little flatter, and keeping your left foot on the ground." He then stepped back and said, "Now don't think about anything and just hit the ball."

As it stood, that was terrible advice. I couldn't think about everything he told me and hit a good shot, and I couldn't think about nothing and hit a good shot. What I needed was to focus on the most important fundamentals until they became automatic and then work on a few more. A next-level philosophy is intended to do the same thing. You just have to make sure that the key concepts receive the majority of your attention. When they do, it's easier to stay centered on what truly matters while giving yourself a platform from which to grow. Without a strong commitment to those fundamentals, neither is possible.

How to Develop a Leadership Philosophy

Know what you want to do (or who you want to be).

The best way to succeed in work or life is to align what you do with what you should be doing. The key is to have a really good understanding of what it is you need to do. Your philosophy will align your behaviors with some level of success or failure. It will only help you succeed if it aligns those behaviors with the things that lead to success. Knowing your goals is a very important first step because your goals frame the path you choose in order to reach them.

Once you know what you want to do or who you want to be, you just have to learn what it takes to get there. That's really the most important step. Philosophy will only bring you closer to your goals if it's based on the principles and fundamentals that lead to their accomplishment. If you want to get the most out of your philosophy, you have to make sure you're crafting it from the most important values and behaviors. From that point, you just have to maintain your focus. It's why Christians aren't asked to study the 110 Commandments. We're asked to focus on the ten most important so we can give them the attention it takes to guide what we do.

Write it down.

I always tell future leaders that one of the most important steps in developing a useable philosophy is writing it down. As you're learning, details can be lost or important points may be forgotten. The written word is more permanent. It's the same reason people write down songs and poems. They don't want to take a chance on losing what they've created, and it helps them commit those things to memory. Thoughts come and go, and it's very hard to build a foundation for your future and your team's direction on something that can come and go.

The best philosophies are a composite of personal beliefs and values, team beliefs and values, and organizational mission. If those aspects are in alignment with your ultimate goals, you will be much more likely to develop successful behaviors. If you can boil those values down to the most important aspects and put them in a written format, you will stand a much greater chance of bringing your goals and behaviors into alignment. It's true for any profession, but especially for leadership. Leadership is a composite of hundreds of skills, so it takes a lot of discipline to continually focus on the most important ones. To write a useable leadership philosophy, follow these simple guidelines:

Step 1: Begin by providing a definition. Do this without using any variation of the words lead, leader, or leadership so you identify its most important aspects. When you define it this way, you have to think about its underlying purpose, and it will help you frame your philosophy.

★ Example: Leadership is the unification of a team around a common goal.

After your definition, insert the following statement: *To be a leader worth following I must adhere to the following principles:*

Steps 2–5 will help you develop a bulleted-type list of the foundational traits and values you consider most important. Step 6 will help you conclude your philosophy.

Step 2: Make one statement about the most important element required to support your organization's mission. This step is designed to help you stay grounded in the principles that will lead your team to success in your chosen field.

★ *Example (for educational leaders): I must uphold the integrity of teaching and learning.*

Step 3: Make one or two statements as to what you believe is the most important aspect of choosing the right direction.

★ *Example: To choose the right direction, I must maintain my awareness of myself, my teammates, and my situation.*

Step 4: Make one or two statements as to what you most value regarding the alignment of work and goals.

★ *Example: To get the most from our efforts, I must carefully plan our goals and our processes.*

Step 5: Make one or two statements of what you believe is most important to building influence with your teammates.

★ *Example: To build influence with others, I must constantly ensure I am worthy of my teammates' trust.*

I must spend time with them to strengthen our relationships.

Step 6: Step six basically concludes your philosophy. Since the purpose of leadership is to add value to the lives of others, you should finish your written work with a final thought regarding what you most want to improve in your teammates' lives. You could begin this conclusion with, "*In the end, I hope...*"

⋆ *Example: In the end, I hope the time I have spent with my team adds value to their lives.*

Philosophy Outline

Leadership is _____ (insert definition)
_____. *To be a leader worth following I must adhere to the following principles:* (insert Steps 2–5)

-

-

-

-

In the end, I hope... (insert Step 6)

Example:

Leadership is the unification of a team around a common goal. To be a leader worth following, I must adhere to the following principles:

- *I must uphold the integrity of teaching and learning.*

- *To choose the right direction, I must maintain my awareness of myself, my teammates, and my situation.*

- *To get the most from our efforts, I must carefully plan our goals and our processes.*

- *To build influence with others, I must constantly ensure I am worthy of my teammates' trust. I must spend time with them to strengthen our relationships.*

In the end, I hope the time I have spent with my team adds value to their lives.

Think about it.

Creating a philosophy is just the first step. What really matters is whether or not you implement those principles and values in your everyday life. The key to making your philosophy a part of you and not just words on a piece of paper is the amount of time you spend thinking about it. Mohandas Gandhi agreed saying, "A man is but the product of his thoughts. What he thinks, he becomes."

For every situation you face in life your thoughts will determine your actions, which will in turn determine your results. As an extension of the SAR Model we discussed in Next-Level Awareness (Situation, Action, Result), I call this the STAR model (Situation, Thought, Action, Results). In any situation quality thoughts drive quality actions; mediocre thoughts drive mediocre actions, and inferior thoughts drive inferior actions. Each set of actions (quality, mediocre, or inferior) would bring equal types of results. If we want to improve those actions, we have to improve our thoughts. The better your philosophy, the more potential you will have for better thoughts. The more you think about that philosophy, the more likely you will reach that potential.

When We Discuss Next-Level Philosophy, We're Really Talking About...

...guidance.

While philosophy does help us choose what to do, it's really about what we choose to be. Your circumstances will always change and anything you do can be affected by thousands of outside influences. If your core beliefs and values change based solely on those variables, you'll find that it's much harder to get where you want to be. That's why our philosophy gives us more control over our circumstances. We don't have to worry about the situation; we just have to focus on how we respond. As Henry Ford observed, "We have always found that if our principles were right, the area over which they were applied did not matter."

The development of strong values and strong habits is even more important during times of crisis. Many times, it's the difficult periods in our life that ultimately determine whether we succeed or fail. I agree with the old Swedish proverb that reads, "Rough waters are truer tests of leadership. In calm water every ship has a good captain." During those rough points the most important question is, "Does the crisis control our behavior, or do we control our behavior?" I've seen far too many people in leadership positions let the crisis dictate their actions. It's almost as if they have no control over their thoughts and responses. It indicates a lack of preparation, but more so a lack of a philosophy to guide them.

I often hear soldiers, nurses, and police officers say that in moments of crisis their training took over and their responses were automatic. That's the level of preparation I want from my nurses, first responders, and soldiers. It's also the preparation I want from my leaders. I want their most important behaviors to be automatic. When you develop a strong philosophy and focus on it every day, your training will take over and you will be the leader you need to be, regardless of the circumstances.

Regarding the guidance philosophy provides, I will leave you with this:

Think purposefully. *Your thoughts become your words.*

Speak carefully. *Your words become your actions.*

Act wisely. *Your actions become your behaviors.*

Behave well. *Your behaviors become you.*

Next-Level Planning

Failing to prepare is preparing to fail.

John Wooden

We've all heard the old saying, "All's well that ends well." I guess it's true, but I don't believe that kind of thinking drives a great deal of success. I want to have a little more control over my outcomes than just waiting for something to end with a positive result. The truth is a lot more things end well that are planned well. When we put more effort into our plans, we can plan to get more from our effort.

I believe in the 5P Mentality: Proper Planning Prevents Poor Performance. As this concept applies to a team, it's another significant responsibility of leadership. If people are going to give you their time and energy, you have an obligation to make good use of both. Great teams must work hard to accomplish their goals, but they have to be working on the right things before any of that effort pays off. If you motivate your teammates to put in 70-hour weeks while going in the wrong direction, you will be further from your goal than if you could only get 30 hours of work going in the right direction.

It seems that nowadays we hear more about the importance of following your passion in life than we do about the importance of planning, but I promise you that passion without a plan only leads to disappointment. It's almost as if we're taught from a young age that all you have to do is follow your passion and success will just fall from the sky. Well, that's just not true, and it's certainly not true for leaders. A passion without a plan is like a destination without a map. You know where you want to go, but you have no idea how to get there.

I constantly hear people talking about how passion and risk-taking are such admirable qualities. They say something like, "Look at Mark Zucherberg. He quit going to school and now he's a billionaire!" Or, "Look at Brad Pitt. He could have been anything, but he took a risk to follow his dream and now he's one of the best actors of our generation!" The thing is that while both men took big risks, they each had a very clear understanding of what they had to do in order to succeed. They did take risks, but they offset those risks with a great deal of talent, education, work, and planning.

The same is true for leadership. We are drawn to confident, passionate leaders because they are often easier to follow. They stir our emotions and get us excited about the future. Without a solid plan, however, that excitement quickly turns to disappointment. Great leaders must have both the passion and the plan. Dr. Martin Luther King, Jr. is an example of such a passionate leader. His speeches may have stirred more emotion than any delivered in American history, but never think for one minute that he wasn't prepared for every single thing he did during the Civil Rights Movement. Every speech aligned with his mission of peaceful resistance and every meeting with public officials laid plans for governmental reform. His passion made his dream accessible, but his plans made his dream achievable.

The key for Dr. King (and any leader) was that he knew his priorities and based his actions, decisions, and speeches on those most important things. A great portion of leading a successful life and a productive team is the ability to set and stick to priorities. When you plan your time according to your priorities, you are more likely to focus on the most important work. Without that plan it's easier to get off track and spend time, energy, and resources on meaningless things. That's why the better we are at planning, the better we are at achieving.

As it relates to leading your team into the future, one of the most important aspects of planning is that it prepares you to take advantage of your opportunities. Bill Gates put that principle to work early in his life. In 1975 he turned an extra-credit assignment at Harvard into the platform for a billion-dollar company. He wanted the assignment to be more meaningful than just a few points added to his final grade, so he designed a rough plan for software that could be used to enhance personal computers. Of course, we know that company today as Microsoft.

Later, when he had an opportunity to make a sales pitch to IBM to provide the software for their personal computers, his planning again allowed him to make the most of his opportunity. It was his attention to detail and his ability to clearly articulate his vision for the two corporations to succeed together that led the IBM executives to give Microsoft the contract.

Of course, we may never prepare for what could be a billion-dollar sales pitch, but it doesn't mean that our goals or our dreams are any less important. Whether it's a change in a product, a new procedure for an assembly line, the construction of a new building, or any of a million decisions to be made by leaders, it's the amount of work you're willing to put into the planning process that will determine the likelihood you and your team will get the results you need.

Next Level: Less Is More

The best way to take planning to the next level is to make it simple. Grand visions are wonderful, but plans must be understood before they can be followed. Many folks think that great plans have to account for every little detail, but the opposite is usually true. It may seem like a contradiction, but to work smarter you have to simplify, not complicate, the things you do. Great plans have to provide parameters and timelines, but to be effective, people have to be able to understand those parameters.

Simpler plans are also usually less prescriptive, which is important if you want great people to do great work. Solid plans should clearly outline the goals, but should allow some flexibility in how people get there. In this way, plans can play to people's strengths and not confine them to one way of thinking or doing.

In times when the world and the work just get busier and busier while teams are asked to do more and more, it should be everyone's goal to be as efficient as possible with time, energy, and resources. Many leaders in manufacturing have adopted a process called Lean Thinking in order to achieve that goal. Lean Thinking is a culture whereby people don't just think about the products they produce; they think about the processes they use during production to ensure they make the most of their time and effort.

It's not just a culture for manufacturing, though. It's really about eliminating waste in all we do from production and service to the way we organize our office. It's a way of conducting business that allows any organization to meet the demands of an ever-changing world by focusing on the efficiency of operations rather than just the effectiveness of the results.

When effectiveness is the goal, you look at the quantity of work that is produced. You may get the results, but you may get them at a higher cost. That point-of-view can lead to wasted time, work, and money. When the focus is on efficiency, however, you still look at the product but also look at the cost/benefit analysis of the process. You have to be aware of what is being done versus what should be or could be done. That point-of-view allows you to get the same results with much less waste.

When plans and processes are streamlined to the point of addressing the most important issues with the appropriate amount of resources, you will find that your team will accomplish more because they will make the most of their time. Plus, when the plan is simple, it's easier to share and easier to understand. At that point the odds greatly increase that your team will know what they need to do and why they need to do it. I do believe in accounting for details, but if the plan is too prescriptive, it may be too constraining. Poor leaders tell great people what to do and how to do it. Great leaders let great people do great work. The plans you set will play a major role in determining which you become.

Where We Go Wrong

We have a plan or a vision, but not both.

The planning process is also where the team decides whether or not they will buy-in to the work, because it's where they decide if they believe in the goal. This is called the vision. The vision is basically the level of connection people feel with the goal they are working to accomplish. If they can see a future that is better or makes more sense, it becomes much easier to do the work that will get them to that place.

I once saw a documentary on Disney World, and the thing that made the biggest impression on me was the way the folks who worked to clean the park approached their jobs. They were happy to do the work even though it was some of the toughest and least glorious. They were engaged, though, because they shared in the vision that it was the "Happiest Place on Earth" and they understood their role in making it that place. Part of the experience the families enjoyed was an immaculately clean environment. Because of that, the custodians didn't focus on the fact that they were picking up trash and cleaning bathrooms. They focused on the role they played in making each family's experience the best it could be.

Just remember that a vision is important, but it's not a plan in and of itself. Visions inspire action. They don't guide action. A vision is only one aspect of the planning process. I think too many people only focus on the "visionary" part when they hear the term visionary leadership. In truth, visionary leadership means that you see a brighter future, but you also have a plan to make sure it happens.

A vision and a plan work together, but shouldn't be confused with one another. Below is a comparison of some of the key differences:

Vision	**Plan**
Broad	Specific
Includes emotion	Sticks to the facts
Paints a picture of success	Draws a blueprint for success
Inspires action	Directs action
Builds buy-in	Builds momentum

Although it's only a part of the planning process, a vision is very important. Vision gives purpose. Without it a team has no reason to strive for their goals. It's that purpose that will bring out the most in your employees. If the team doesn't see or understand the vision, they will not be as motivated in its pursuit. Plans make achievement possible, but visions make plans purposeful.

We miss the little things that make a big difference.

The planning process truly is a process. We all want to accomplish big things in our lives, but the key to "big" success is to continually engage in a process of getting bigger. We don't just wake up one morning and find that we're successful. Achieving a worthwhile goal is only possible by doing the little things each day. Only through many footsteps can we get to the end of a long journey. We just have to plan so we make the most of each step.

The best leaders know that the greatest achievements are accomplished by attention to the smallest details. I think Benjamin Franklin summed it up pretty well when he wrote, "A little neglect may bring a lot of mischief. For want of a nail the shoe was lost; for want of a shoe the horse was lost; for want of a horse the rider was lost; and for want of a rider the battle was lost." You may want to be remembered as a leader who accomplished big things, but you will never do big things if you don't remember to take care of the little ones.

Now remember, I'm not talking about planning every single thing your teammates will do. I'm talking about raising your level of awareness regarding the little things so that your goals and plans make sense. Details help you be accurate, and when you're planning, accuracy is very important. You have to check your facts, no matter how confident you are in what you know.

For example, if I told you the sun rises in the east and sets in the west, you may feel pretty confident that it was a true statement. Would you check the facts, anyway? You could verify the direction by taking a compass outside in the morning and again in the evening to see for yourself. At that point you could be certain of the direction. Technically, however, the statement would still be wrong. The sun doesn't rise. It's in a constant position. The Earth rotates making the sun appear to rise. If your team was depending on you to be precise, you may have let them down by missing that one detail.

We don't use our imagination.

Imagination is very important to planning. Albert Einstein once said, "Logic will get you from A to B. Imagination will take you everywhere else." When we plan, we are dealing with events that have yet to happen, and as we set goals, we are basically imagining a better future. The better we are at imagining that future and what it will take to get there, the better our chances of developing a plan that aligns our present actions with our future desires. I've often heard that you have to see it before you can believe it, but I think we also have to see it before we can achieve it.

The key to a good leadership imagination is knowing enough about your team and their capabilities to imagine how they will interact and perform over the course of our plans. If we dream up a great plan but the pieces don't fit with our team, we may just be setting everyone up for failure. As we have said, leadership is not about you; it's about your effect. The same principle applies to the planning process. It's not about the plan. It's about the plan's effect on the people you lead.

How To Build Better Plans

Make sure the goal makes sense.

Planning is tough, but we can make it easier by setting better goals. If the goal makes sense, it's much easier for the plan to fall into place. To do that, you just have to begin with the end in mind. When you and your team have a clear picture of where you want to be, you can work to align your plans and your actions with those goals. Without clear goals, meaningless work starts creeping into our daily routine and it becomes easier to spend time on those unimportant things.

I advise setting GREAT Goals in order to keep everyone focused on what truly matters. In order to make a difference, goals must be Grounded, Relevant, Engaging, Assessable, and Timely.

Grounded: Goals must be grounded in reality or they will just frustrate you and your team. Any goal must take into account the capabilities of the people and the resources available to them. If a goal isn't achievable, no plan will be successful. More importantly, no team will be successful.

Relevant: People have to know the goal they're working toward has a purpose. If the goal has no purpose, the work has no purpose, and no one wants to waste their time doing irrelevant work. Goals can be vague in the boardroom, but they must be purposeful in the workroom.

Engaging: Goals often make sense to boards and CEOs, but unless they make sense to the individuals doing the work, it's really hard for them to be engaged in what they do. Only the goals that connect with the employees are goals that will motivate their performance.

Assessable: Peter Drucker, often referred to as the Father of Modern Management, once advised, "If you can't measure it, you can't manage it." The key to setting measurable goals is to set specific goals. Setting a goal to improve customer service is nice, but vague. Setting a goal to return every phone call or email within 24 hours is precise and measurable.

Timely: Defining time limits is very important when setting goals. The only difference between a dream and a goal is a deadline. Dreamers want to succeed. Planners know when they'll do it.

At its most basic level, a plan is a set of steps you put in place to accomplish something. The trick is planning the last step before you ever take the first one. You have to know your goal before you can design a plan to help you reach it. A plan is a path, but without a good destination, it could be a path to nowhere. The better you define your team's destination, the more likely you will be able to plan a way to achieve it. Clear goals lead to clear plans. Shaky goals lead to shaky plans.

Involve a diverse group of people.

For just about every situation we face in life and leadership, the right choice exists. We just have to realize that it may not exist in our mind or our experience. As Shakespeare wrote in *Hamlet,* "There are more things in Heaven and Earth, Horatio, Than are dreamt of in your philosophy." You just have to decide whether you feel it's your job to come up with the best decision, or your job to find it. If you believe that your job is to find it, you will let others help. That's when you'll truly take your planning skills to the next level. Involving different people with different experiences is the key to successful plans.

We want diversity in our teams and our planning processes for the same reason we want diversity in our financial portfolio. If you put all of your money in one stock, you're in trouble if that stock crashes. If you put all of your money in a diverse array of stocks, bonds, funds, and securities, however, you'll be much safer. The same goes for planning. Surround yourself with like-minded people with similar experiences and you'll be in trouble if the circumstances change beyond your scope of reference. When you involve a group of people from different departments and different backgrounds, however, you'll bring a lot more experience to the table and be better prepared for a variety of situations.

Diversity is not just a mandate to include different cultures and races in the workplace. It's an effort to broaden your perspective. The more diverse perspectives and opinions you collect, the better equipped you will be to make decisions that work for everyone. Many leaders think they are not doing their job if they are not the one coming up with the plan, but that line of thinking leads to plans developed from just one perspective. What I have discovered is that while I usually have to approve the plan, I don't have to develop it. It not only takes a lot of pressure off of me to come up with the right plan, but it increases the odds that we actually will.

Expect problems along the way.

Too many times I've seen people fail with their plans because they allowed their plans to fail. Many times we find that once we get started, things aren't quite what we imagined they would be. It's actually a very common scenario. For instance, think of all the marketing and PR firms around 1989 who made ten-year plans for communication. They most likely considered all the newest technologies like car phones, fax machines, and word processing software. If they weren't willing to change along the way, however, they would have been dead in the water when the Internet exploded just a few years later.

That's why the best planners are willing to adjust their plans. I often use the term *navigation* when discussing leadership for this very reason. Navigators aren't interested in being right from the start. They're interested in getting to the right place in the end. Those leaders aren't afraid to change their plans if they see it's in everyone's best interest to do so. John Maxwell certainly agrees. Early in his career he wrote an acronym for the words "PLAN AHEAD." It stands for:

Predetermine your course of action

Lay out your goals

Allow time for adjustment

Notify key personnel

Allow time for acceptance

Head into action

Expect problems

Always point to your successes

Daily, review your progress

Notice that four of the nine points in this guide highlight to the need to review and/or change your plans. Making adjustments, allowing for acceptance, expecting problems, and reviewing progress are all efforts to ensure the plan is working as it should. These are the marks of great leaders in the planning and navigation processes. Narrow-minded leaders set plans in stone and then expect their people to push through any barrier. Open-minded leaders are willing to change course when it becomes necessary. Which would you prefer to follow?

When All Is Said and Done, Next-Level Planning Is...

...potential.

Without a solid plan, you severely limit your team's potential. All the talent in the world can't save a team that's going in the wrong direction or doing the wrong work. Admiral Hyman Rickover, who is often referred to as the father of the nuclear Navy, once told a group of newly promoted officers, "Organizations don't get things done. Plans and programs don't get things done. Only people get things done. Organizations, plans, and programs either help or hinder people."

Our teammates want to be successful. Most of them even have the ability to do it. It's just that many times they don't know how to go about getting there. A leader's job is to help them see where they need to be, then help them navigate the path. In other words, it's the leader's job to know where people need to be, then provide a plan to make it possible. That's the true value of planning. We make plans so we make it easier on our teammates to succeed.

Remember, your effectiveness as a manager may be determined by whether or not you got the job done, but your effectiveness as a leader will be determined by whether or not your teammates did all they were capable of doing. When you make the most of your planning processes, you will be much more likely to help your teammates do more than just set their goals. You will help them set their potential.

Next-Level Decision-Making

None of us are as smart as all of us.

Peter Grazier

I believe one of the biggest differences between leaders and follow-ers is often the willingness or ability to make decisions. One of the first questions I always ask new leaders is, "Would you rather make decisions or have them made for you?" It's a very important question. A lot of people would much rather have someone tell them what to do so they can just get to work. There's nothing wrong with that and we need those people, but it's a luxury leaders can't afford.

Planning is an important phase in the process of choosing the right direction, but it's only one step. Once the work begins your team will need a leader who can make decisions to continually guide their action. While your plans may set your team's potential, your decisions determine whether or not they'll reach it. If you want to have an impact on the future, you have to decide where to go and how to get there. It's the only way to have any control over where you go. The best way to control your future is to create it, but if you're not willing to make decisions, you'll never get past the present.

Just being willing to *make* decisions, though, does not mean you will be a great leader. The quality of your leadership will depend on the quality of those decisions. If your decisions consistently align with your team's long-range plans, you'll be more likely to get everyone where they need to be. You just have to make sure the decisions you make are based on the needs of the organization and your teammates.

To lead, you have to change your perspective. As a machinist, your viewpoint is defined by the parameters of your job on a particular machine. As a unit leader, your viewpoint may be several machines. As a floor manager, you may have to include many machines and the supply chain. As a plant manager, you may oversee all machines, all suppliers, HR, Finance, quality control, etc. As you advance in your career, your decisions will affect the lives and work of more and more people. You just have to remember that those decisions are not made for you and the moment. They are made for your team and their future.

Every time you make a decision you're setting a new direction for everyone who follows you. Decision-making is one of the toughest jobs a leader will do. It's too big, in fact, for anyone to do by themselves. Personally, I like to think of my role as less of a decision-maker and more of an option-selector. I'm not nearly smart enough to come up with the right answers every time, but I do believe that the right decision is out there somewhere. When you involve other people, you tap into more experience and more information, which means you increase your odds of finding the best choice. I've found that the more advice I get before making a decision, the easier it is for me to make the right call. If you're willing to include others you have an arsenal of limitless experience. If your mind's already made up, all you have is your own.

We have to reach a level of what I like to call "Decisional Maturity" before we truly start making the best decisions. Decisional Maturity happens when you start making decisions based on what is best, not necessarily what you think is best. Always remember that in the end, *who* is right never matters as much as *what* is right.

Your teammates have a very big stake in the decisions you make. Pastor Gerald Brooks believes, "When you become a leader, you give up your right to think about yourself." The more you keep that in mind, the more likely you will make decisions that make sense and the more likely your team will make the best of the decisions you make.

Taking It to the Next Level: Managing Decisions

Decision-making is a tough element because it takes place in the present but has an effect on the future. In that regard, we shouldn't worry as much about what we do when the decision is made, but what we do afterwards. While we should always make every effort to make the best decisions and commit to our direction, we have a responsibility to change course if we begin to see that there may be a better way. As Elvis Presley once said, "If things are going wrong, don't go with them." You see, success is not as much about making decisions as it is about making decisions work. Anyone can make a decision. Leaders manage them.

Managing decisions requires two things: an awareness of what has happened as a result of our choices and a willingness to change if necessary. If you want to make the most of everyone's time and effort, you have to know what's being done and be willing to alter your decision if things go wrong. Doing so will mean that you are much more likely to get the results you want because it means that your entire future is not riding on the first call you made. Inflexible decision-makers give themselves one chance to get it right. Flexible decision-makers give themselves many chances.

A willingness to change your mind doesn't just make it easier for you to get good results, though. It makes it easier for everyone else to follow your lead. When others know you are willing to alter a decision, it will be much easier for them to get on board in the beginning because they'll know you won't make them stick to a bad plan. You'll also gain more influence with the team because they'll know you're in it for them, not for you.

It can be very hard to change your mind, but without that willingness, you put all your future eggs in one decision basket. You can make it easier on yourself, though. All you have to do is become comfortable with occasionally being wrong. One of my greatest mentors, Ed Story, always told me, "Juston, when it's time to make a decision, make it and move on. If it's the wrong decision, just admit it and fix it." I can't tell you how much easier that philosophy has made my life, and it can work for you, too. You just have to decide which you would prefer as a final result of your decisions: your decision, or the best decision. The former means you always have to be right. The latter means you just have to do what's right.

Where We Go Wrong

We fear commitment.

It's not easy being a decision-maker, and quite frankly many people have trouble with the concept. A decision is a commitment, and if you're not willing to make that commitment, you can't make a decision. Of course, that means you can't be a leader. Too many people will depend on you for direction to avoid that duty. That's why Abraham Lincoln advised, "You cannot escape the responsibility of tomorrow by evading it today." Leaders usher people toward tomorrow; therefore, they have to make decisions in the present.

Sometimes, though, it's not just a fear of commitment that keeps a leader from making a decision, it's a desire to only commit to the perfect choice. Many times the tendency is to become so obsessed with every little detail or every possible outcome that we never make a choice. You have to operate between what Eric Harvey and Alexander Lucia call the Kneejerk Reaction and Paralysis of Analysis. You can't commit too quickly and you can't keep everyone waiting indefinitely. We always want to collect as much information and feedback as possible, but eventually we have to choose one direction so we can unify everyone else's.

Our short-term decisions don't align with our long-term goals.

Long-term goals are usually the significant ones that make a big difference for a person, team, or organization. What makes them difficult is that they also require consistent attention over a long period of time. American writer Alvin Toffler says, "You've got to think about big things while you're doing small things, so that all the small things go in the right direction." Long-term goals must guide short-term decisions if you expect to get the results you want. For instance, if you're saving for a new house you can't buy a new car every two years, or if you're trying to lose 15 pounds, you can't have pizza and wings every Thursday night.

It's really a matter of focus. If you continually focus on your most important goals you will handle the day-to-day business while staying grounded in the work that truly matters. Without a strong commitment to that vision, it's just too easy to get caught up in the immediate needs. Sadly, that lack of focus is a very common occurrence. Many great ideas have died on the vine because after an implementation meeting, managers and team leaders shift their attention to other day-to-day issues.

Leaders can't make all of their decisions based on what's happening at that moment. It's an easy trap to fall into because the here-and-now can dominate your time. Before you know it, though, six months have passed and the team hasn't accomplished anything that would truly make a difference. It's not always easy to keep your focus on a long range plan but anything worthwhile requires that effort. My best advice is to begin each day by reviewing your most important goals so you will be more likely to focus on their completion. If you do, you will find it much easier to add value to all of your short-term work because it will actually lead to the accomplishment of your long-term goals.

We don't seek feedback.

Have you ever said, "I wish I would have thought of that?" Sure. We all have. It usually applies to something that could have made us a lot of money or saved us a lot of time. There's another way of looking at it, though. It's also a reminder that we don't know it all and that we'll never think of everything. If we're not willing to include others in our decision-making processes, we may just be losing out on a lot of great ideas that someone else would have thought of.

How well you collect feedback in the decision-making process will often determine how well you make decisions. The trick is finding a way to get from feedback to decision. If you're trying to collect feedback from a team of three, it's not hard to let every team member tell you what they think and take their suggestions into consideration. Plus, once the decision is made, you can easily keep everyone in the loop during the process and explain why you made your choice. If you're trying to collect and share information with a team of 300 people, it can be a different story.

When working with large teams, I've found that it's often easier to just go ahead and throw an idea out there and let people pick it apart; other times I've formed small workgroups to come up with options. However you do it, though, it's always a good idea to let others help. Just make sure that if you ask for input, you're willing to receive it. There's only one thing worse than not asking for the opinion of others: asking for it and then consistently ignoring it.

How To Be Better Decision-Makers

Get all the facts.

Decision-making isn't easy. It takes a lot of time and a lot of thought to gain the awareness you'll need to make the best decisions. President Harry Truman understood that concept. Anytime someone came to him for a decision, one of his first questions was always, "How much time do I have?" He wanted to make sure that he could do the best job he could do, so he made sure he took time to collect all of the information that would allow him to make the best decision.

Your decisions will only be as good as the information you have, not the assumptions you make or the wishes you wish. Colin Powell thought he had reliable information when he announced to the United Nations that Iraq and Saddam Hussein had weapons of mass destruction. The editors of *The Chicago Daily Tribune* thought they had accurate information when they ran the headline, "Dewey Defeats Truman" after the 1948 Presidential election (Truman won, by the way). In both cases the decisions were flawed because the information was flawed.

I used to say that there are two sides to every story. After many years in administration, I now say that there are *at least* two sides to every story. With all those stories floating around, it's easy to jump on someone else's misperception, and it's really dangerous when opinion becomes fact with no justification. People may not intend to deceive you, but they may not have the whole story, themselves. When people bring me information, the first thing I want to know is, "How are you sure?" As W. Edwards Deming once said, "In God we trust. All others bring data."

I have to admit that when I started my Ph.D. program I didn't think it would add a great deal of value to my life, but it did more to improve my decision-making abilities than any training I've ever received. You see, researchers want to uncover new facts, but in order to be considered valid, those facts must be put through a rigorous set of checks and balances to ensure their accuracy. One of the methods used to verify information is called triangulation. Basically, triangulation means that unless you can verify what you find using three different methods or three different sources, you can't consider it reliable.

If you train yourself to do the same, you'll find that your ability to make quality decisions drastically improves because the quality of your information drastically improves. For example, I once considered establishing an extension campus in a remote area of our college's service region based on one group's recommendation and data. When I also asked for population numbers from another source and looked at college attendance trends from yet another, it was clear that the campus was not viable. Furthermore, some of the first data turned out to be flawed. If I had made my decision based on that first recommendation, I would have made a big mistake.

It doesn't matter if you're talking about work decisions, career options, or how to invest your money, building a habit of using multiple sources of information will greatly increase your chances of choosing better directions. In fact, I've gotten to the point that I use the triangulation approach when any information comes to me, even if it's a trusted source. Doing so means I'll be more likely to base my decisions on judgment or facts instead of jumping on someone else's ill-gained conclusions.

Ask more questions.

My first piece of decision-making advice to new leaders is always the same: ask a lot of questions. Many leaders tend to focus more on answers than they do questions, but questions are actually the most important part of the decision-making equation. Think about it this way: how much more would you know right now if you had a very good question every time someone asked, "Any questions?" Now think about how that resulting knowledge would impact your ability to make quality decisions.

Questions aren't asked to generate answers. They're asked to generate awareness. That awareness leads to options, and options are really what we should seek. It's why the late Reverend Robert H. Schuller had this advice: "When you've exhausted all possibilities, remember this: You haven't!" When you place a priority on asking questions, you'll be looking for other possibilities. When you place a priority on providing answers, you'll be limiting yourself to the ones you already have. Answers only give you one way to solve a problem. Options are limitless.

Remove emotion from the process.

Successful decisions require two basic elements: getting them right and getting everyone else on board. Emotional decisions rarely accomplish either. Your personal emotions do nothing to help you make better decisions for others. The choices leaders make affect many lives; therefore, we owe it to all of them to make the most of each choice. Emotional decisions are usually uninformed, incorrect, or hasty. They are the ones you're more likely to regret, put you in a corner, or make you look like a fool. Plus, when you act out of emotion you are more likely to put everyone else in a defensive position, and that's the last thing you want when you are trying to unify direction. Even perfect decisions are useless if people aren't willing to embrace them.

The greatest decision-makers are highly objective, with no personal agenda. To be the best decision-maker you can be, you have to separate fact from emotion. Facts should influence emotion, not the other way around. When people are able to focus on decisions without being influenced by their pride or personal feelings, they can focus on finding the best way to do things. Too many leaders get emotionally attached to a decision and their energy is focused on "their way." When that happens, those leaders try to protect their interests instead of looking out for everyone else's.

Make your decision.

Before any decision can be the right decision, you have to make it. When you have listened to all the opinions, gathered all the facts, and considered all the options, the only thing left to do is make your choice. No one can make progress or unify their direction until you do.

George Washington offered a great example of the unity confident decision-makers can provide with his crossing of the Delaware River during the Revolutionary War. Washington and his Continental Army had just been driven out of New York and New Jersey. He was outmanned, outgunned, and most of his soldiers just wanted to go home. In fact, most of the American public was beginning to believe they should forget about independence and just remain under British control. At that point, things were not looking good for America's Revolutionary efforts.

Washington, however, refused to give up. He knew that if he could find a way to cross the Delaware, he could catch the British army by surprise and get a foothold in Trenton. The problem was that all of his advisors told him he couldn't safely get his army across. It was late in December and there were large chunks of ice on the river. Since the ice didn't move until dark, the crossing would have to take place at night.

Regardless, General Washington was convinced that it was the right thing to do. So he chose to do it, and he did it with conviction. His confidence inspired the other soldiers to believe in his choice, so they all believed in the direction their leader had chosen. Once crossed, the soldiers attacked Trenton and quickly won because of the surprise. The battle was one of the most significant turning points in the war, but it would have never happened without Washington's ability to make a call.

At the End of the Day, Next-Level Decision Making Is...

...thinking.

Decisions are not made by thinking in the moment. Decisions are made by thinking constantly. Napoleon Bonaparte once responded to a question regarding his legendary preparation by saying, "If I always appear prepared, it is because I have meditated long and have foreseen what may occur. It is not genius which reveals to me suddenly and secretly what I should do in circumstances unexpected by others; it is thought and preparation."

There are basically two types of decision-making processes: those that require long-term thought and those that require short-term thought. Nobel Prize winning psychologist Daniel Kahneman calls this Thinking Fast and Thinking Slow. Thinking fast refers to automatic responses. For instance, if I asked you to provide an answer for $2 + 2$ you would automatically recognize the answer as 4. You wouldn't have to take time to formulate a response. Thinking slow, however, is a little more involved. If I asked you to provide an answer for 48×37.5, I doubt anything would automatically come to mind. You would have to dedicate a bit more thought to that answer.

Thinking Fast and Thinking Slow is more than just providing answers to math problems, though. It's really about taking a look at which system drives our decisions. For leaders, a lot of our decisions should come from efforts to think slow, but what Kahneman and many other researchers have found is that people prefer to think fast because it's so much easier. The thing is, leadership decisions aren't easy. Even the ones that have to be made fast require a lot of awareness and prior thought.

That's why the greatest leaders I know spend a lot of time in reflection. When you spend time reflecting on the things you have seen, heard, and done, you are basically practicing your decision-making skills. This not only improves your ability to think slow, but your ability to think well. When you constantly examine what you and others have done right and wrong in the past, you have a much better idea of what to do in the future.

There are basically three levels of reflective thought. The three levels of reflection as I see them are:

1. **Remembering**

   Remembering an event is an important first step in reflection, but just provides a picture of prior events. Remembering is important because it allows us to keep a log of what has worked and what has not worked. It's not experience, though, because it just deals with the past.

2. **Connection**

   To find the meaning in any event we must process our memories in a way that allows us to make connections with what we know. Otherwise, we have no way to understand it. Reflective thought allows us to use our prior understanding to connect with new knowledge. This level of reflection is more directly tied to our present.

3. **Active Reflection**

If you actively imagine what was done and what could have been done differently, you are preparing for what you will do in the future. Active reflection means that you are putting yourself in the situation so you can practice. It's how we turn past experience into future insight.

In the end, the experience we gain through reflection allows us to become better decision-makers. As we've discussed, decision-making is an activity in the present that has an impact on the future. Since the future hasn't happened yet, the only way we can increase our odds of making positive decisions is to learn enough to have a really good idea of what will happen once they're made. Through reflection, we evaluate the past and learn in the present so we can plan for the future.

Aligning Work with Goals

Leadership must set direction,
but to be effective it must inspire action.

Next-Level Alignment

Alignment is not about the management of quality.
It is about the quality of management.

Takeo Shimina

Have you ever felt like there were times in your life that you were busy accomplishing nothing? If you have, those were most likely the times when you were out of alignment. In other words, your actions didn't align with your goals. You see, there are thousands of things we could spend our time doing each day, but only a few of them will get us where we truly want to be.

The same principle applies to leading the time and effort of others. All of the things you and your team do throughout the course of a day will either go toward the accomplishment of goals or they won't. If they do, you will be much more likely to succeed. If they don't, you will be much more likely to fail. It's a pretty simple formula, really.

Sometimes leaders and companies learn this lesson the hard way, though. Texas Instruments used to be one of the strongest technology companies in America. They had a great niche in the market and put out a strong product, especially the handheld calculator. During the 1980s, though, they decided it was time to get into the personal computer business. They developed a device that exceeded the industry standards and won several design awards. It was a marvel of technology. So why haven't you heard about the Texas Instrument personal computer? Well, it wasn't user friendly and the customers wouldn't buy it. The company aligned the product with its purpose but didn't align the product with consumer needs, so they failed with one of the best personal computers ever built.

Basically, there are five types of alignment that must be addressed. Leaders must ensure that the situation, mission, goals, work, and people align with one another so that the mission makes sense, the goals support the mission, the work accomplishes the goals, and the people do the work. Sounds easy, right? The problem is that it gets really complicated when you have multiple people and multiple departments working toward multiple goals. In that environment, alignment doesn't just happen naturally. That type of alignment takes leadership.

The image below represents the five aspects of alignment.

Total Alignment

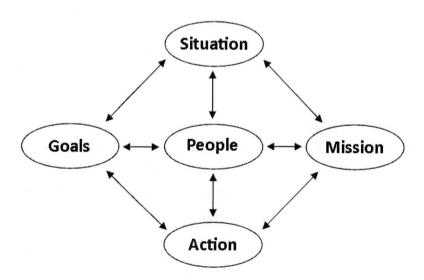

Alignment is the leadership element that keeps us from straying from our purpose. It ensures from top to bottom that the work being done is leading to personal and organizational success. Without it, we have no way of knowing that what we do today is going to have a positive impact on tomorrow. When organizations get out of alignment they run the risk of disconnecting from their people or their products.

For example, there was a time when Kmart outperformed Wal-Mart in the discount retail business. The Kmart brand operated more stores in more states and moved a much greater volume of merchandise. That is, until Kmart started moving into specialized retail enterprises like clothing and jewelry stores. They began to stray from their central purpose and devoted too much time, energy, and resources to other interests. Meanwhile Wal-Mart was completely focused on perfecting the processes and services of its core business. Before long, Wal-Mart had taken the number one spot in the market and Kmart's stock price had plummeted.

Floyd Hall took over as CEO of the company in 1996 and changed all of that by returning their focus to the core retail business and the needs of the customer. He worked toward the total alignment of the Kmart brand with a product the customer wanted and made sure the employees did the work that supported that mission. He even based half of the store managers' bonuses on customer satisfaction ratings. Soon, the stock prices had recovered by 65%. Unfortunately, that brief period of misalignment was enough to prevent them from ever being the king of discount retail again.

The great thing about alignment is that the closer you come to aligning the managerial operations of your organization, the more time you can spend developing employees, touching base with customers, and devoting time to future plans. That's how teams truly reach the next level. They align their situation, mission, and work, and then get better at doing the work. When you can spend the majority of your time supporting the growth of your employees there's no limit to what everyone can accomplish, but it's impossible to do that without the structure and organization that alignment brings.

Taking it to the Next Level: Building Positive Momentum

Nothing will have a bigger impact on your ability to align your team's work and goals than the group of leaders you have helping you lead the people and the processes. They are the ones who will build or kill your initiatives by either building or killing your momentum. If that group is strong, your team will be unified in a singular direction and much more likely to spend their time working on the right things. If that group is weak, your team will be less likely to do the right work.

In any team or organization, you will usually have three groups of people: those who provide positive leadership, those who provide negative leadership, and those who look for someone to lead them. The people who provide positive leadership most likely want to do right by you and the company; therefore, they will want to work toward accomplishing team objectives. The second group can be just as influential, but nowhere near as constructive. They usually want to do something that strays from the unification of work and goals. Of course, the third group will gravitate toward one of the first two.

I used to spend a great deal of my time with the negative leaders thinking I would eventually bring them on board. What I have learned over the years, however, is that my time is much better spent with the positive leaders. When that group is supported and empowered to do good work, eventually their attitude and success will spread to the majority of the team, especially those who are looking for someone to lead them. It's that type of positive momentum you want to build.

As the size of the teams you lead grows, you will find it increasingly difficult to spend time with each and every employee. It's the leaders around you that will ultimately determine how that work gets done, and how the rest of the people feel about doing it. The more time you invest in training and connecting with those positive leaders, the better equipped they will be to help you keep the team's work aligned with their goals.

Alignment is far too big of a job to do alone. Even Jesus had the disciples, and he continually worked to make sure they understood their purpose and that they had the skills they needed to do their jobs. Leaders who try to do everything by themselves struggle with alignment. Coincidentally (or not), it's those teams who also struggle with their leader.

Where We Go Wrong

We have a lack of awareness.

To align people, processes, work, and goals, you have to know a lot about people, processes, work, and goals. It takes a lot of effort to do that. When you make decisions about how other people need to spend their time in order to maximize profit or achieve organizational objectives, you have to know more than just the market or a strategic plan. You also have to know what your teammates are doing and what they are capable of doing.

Staying aligned to an ever-changing environment means constantly making sure what you provide is really what you need to produce and that everyone's work is focused on that product. Companies like Wal-Mart and FedEx receive daily, not monthly or quarterly, reports on what the customer wants so they can be sure to deliver it. When Sam Walton walked into any Wal-Mart store, one of the first questions he would ask his manager was, "What's selling today?" He wanted to know the market condition, but more importantly, he wanted to know if his leader was in touch with the situation.

Consistent two-way communication is vital to maintaining your awareness for the purpose of alignment. If you're not getting feedback from your team, your decisions may be setting everyone up for failure. Sir Clowdisley Shovell, who commanded a fleet of British ships in 1707, lost his bearings off the coast of Sicily one cloudy night. He thought he was heading out to open seas and refused to listen to anyone who was telling him differently. In fact, he had a seaman hanged for speaking against his decision to press on through the darkness.

He would have done well to have listened, though. Because of his closed-mindedness and lack of awareness, he lost four ships and 2000 men when he ran the fleet into the rocks just off shore. It was the worst accident in British naval history, and could have been avoided if Captain Shovell would have let others help keep him informed. Conventional wisdom says that knowing is half the battle. For leaders, it may be more like 75-90%.

We make everything the most important thing.

When everything becomes the most important thing, it's impossible to align work and goals. One of the most critical aspects of alignment is setting priorities for everyone's work. Otherwise they may spend equal time and energy on menial tasks as they spend on key strategic initiatives. For most people, there are many jobs that could be done at any given time, so they need someone to help them make sure they are doing the most important ones first. When we have no priorities it's like mixing ten jigsaw puzzles and trying to put them together. The work is frustrating, more difficult than it should be, and takes a lot longer to get done.

I once worked in an organization that operated under those circumstances. We had strategic goals that were considered to be the most important services of our institution, but anything that crossed our leader's desk became the most important thing in the moment. Every week there was a new initiative or a new project that was supposed to be our top priority. Because of that culture, we never got very far on the things that mattered most because we were constantly spending our time working on the new priority. The trouble is, when everything is the most important thing, nothing is important. As expected, we finished that year completing 20 mediocre projects instead of five great ones.

We don't confront problems with alignment early enough.

You have to know where your team stands each day as you progress toward your goals to make sure everyone is going in the right direction. In fact, it's more important to know that your team is moving the right way than it is to know whether or not they're moving, at all. When no work is done on any given day, it means it will take one day longer to accomplish your objectives. When the wrong work is done on any given day, it could take much more time to recover because the team has gone in the wrong direction. The longer everyone goes down that path, the longer it will take to get back on track. Misalignment is easier to solve in the earliest stages before things drift too far apart. Oftentimes, this calls for some type of confrontation regarding problem behaviors, poor performance, wasted time, or misplaced priorities.

Leaders who avoid these problems don't solve them. It's human nature to want to avoid confrontation, especially among your coworkers, but the longer a problem goes unaddressed the harder it is to solve and the further out of alignment the team becomes. Even worse, until they're confronted, those problems may just continue to grow. Avoiding problems makes them part of the future. Addressing problems makes them part of the past.

How to Do Better

Keep your eyes on the prize.

Alignment is really a set of choices. We choose our goals, and we choose what we do to accomplish them. For the most part, teams and organizations will stand a really good chance of succeeding if everyone makes decisions that align their short-term actions with their long-term goals. In other words, it's about aligning macro and micro decisions. Large-scale (or macro) decisions are the ones that set the overarching goals for a team or organization. Small-scale (or micro) decisions take place when deciding how to accomplish those goals. It's important to understand the difference between micro and macro decisions and their place amongst the team in order to lead both short-term and long-term work.

Micro Decisions: Micro decisions are basically the short-term choices we need to make in order to do our jobs. While individual team members may be aware of long-range initiatives (and may even support those initiatives), their work is still their primary concern. The majority of your teammates will most likely identify with their job and the micro decisions that affect it. They may very well love the company and support its mission, but the short-term work is their most immediate concern.

Macro Decisions: Macro decisions are the choices that affect long-term success such as setting quarterly goals or strategic initiatives. Strategic plans are important to any team or organization because they keep us relevant to the environment and prepared for the future. However, it's often easy for leaders (especially senior-level leaders) to overlook individual concerns when making macro decisions. Leaders must be aware of how their decisions affect the individuals on the team so the employees have an easier time aligning their work with the plan.

Everyone must understand that short-term work only has value if it leads to long-term significance. That can only happen if we are aligning our micro decisions and daily effort with an important long-range goal. It's the amount of attention we give to that goal each day that determines our ultimate success. I think Jim Barksdale, former CEO of Netscape, said it best when he told his employees, "The main thing is to keep the main thing, the main thing." Leaders must give consistent attention to long-term goals if they are to ensure that the short-term work adds the most value to the organization. Of course, when you align the work your employees do with the most valuable objectives of the company, you don't just make the work more meaningful; you make the employee more valuable. And that's the real main thing.

Get everything in order.

The best way to ensure the alignment of work, goals, and environment is to be highly organized. People and processes usually don't just naturally align in the chaos of the world in which we operate. Leaders must work very hard to create the type of culture and procedures that make alignment possible. George Labovitz and Victor Rosansky have made a career out of helping leaders do that very thing. They lead a very successful consulting firm and have worked with some of the best companies in the world to help them bring their operations into alignment. They have made a difference for hundreds of companies by providing structure and order to teams and organizations. At the beginning of every job, they advise the following six steps:

- Start with the main thing

- Create success indicators

- Link goals, work, and rewards

- Make sure everyone has goals that relate to the main thing

- Train people to do the job they need to do

- Review performance regularly

Leaders who adhere to the structure provided by those steps will be more likely to create a system whereby everyone feels secure in what they do, what they should do, and why they do it. Supervisors will have a plan to ensure the alignment of work and goals and employees won't have to worry about whether or not they're going in the right direction. It takes a lot of time and energy to organize processes and people, but in the end, organized work is efficient work. And efficiency is the name of the alignment game.

Align your support with everyone else's work.

Another aspect of alignment is the connection between support and work. I discovered this while working for a small construction company in Southeastern Kentucky. The owner was a great guy, but really didn't know what it took to support his employees. If we'd ask for a sledge hammer he'd bring us a jackhammer. If we needed a small hacksaw he'd buy us a power saw. He was only trying to help by providing more than what we had asked for, but the fact was we didn't need a jackhammer and a power saw; we needed a sledge hammer and a hacksaw.

One of our most common jobs was laying a one to two inch water line for coal companies between their work sites. We told the boss that if he purchased a Ditch Witch (a machine that digs deep, narrow trenches), we could lay the pipe much faster and save enough time to easily bid more jobs. One week later, the boss brought us a new excavator with a three-foot wide bucket. He was proud of his brand new machine, but all it did was make more work for us. The Ditch Witch was a tool designed to dig deep, narrow trenches that were easy to cover up once the pipe was laid. The excavator dug a HUGE trench which meant it took us five times longer to fill back in.

Leaders can't assume they know what their teammates need more than their teammates know what they need. We have to understand the situation and the people well enough to know what type of support is necessary, not just what we think is necessary. We want to support our teammates' opportunities to grow and achieve, but if we don't align the opportunity with the support we're not providing opportunity. We're providing frustration.

In the End, Next-Level Alignment Is...

...management.

I don't believe that management in and of itself is leadership, but alignment is a very important managerial function designed to ensure that our efforts are successful. I don't think it's enough to just lead a team to accomplish their goals if we want the best for them. To add the most value to their lives we have to reach those goals as efficiently as possible. Otherwise you're robbing the people of their time and limiting their potential. I mean, if you accomplish a goal in one year that could have only taken nine months, isn't it irresponsible to take one year?

We never have complete control over our success, but efforts made to align our goals and the environment followed by efforts made to align our work with those goals is about the closest we can come. Every choice we make will either serve to bring us closer to the things we want and need or take us further from them. Alignment is a lot like the first rule of geometry: the shortest distance between two points is a straight line. When our efforts are aligned with our goals, we are on a straight path toward them. When our efforts do not align with our goals we increase the distance between the two points.

If you want to help your team succeed, you have to help them come into alignment. Sometimes that means making a decision; sometimes it means providing structure and organization; and sometimes it means feedback and confrontation. These managerial duties are strong elements of successful leadership. I have always heard that all leaders are managers, but not all managers are leaders. Both roles are important, though. Leadership provides the vision and influence to motivate people to move. Management provides the plan and the structure to make sure everyone moves in the right direction. I think Stephen Covey said it best when he wrote, "Effective leadership is putting first things first. Effective management is discipline, carrying it out."

Next-Level Communication

How well we communicate is not determined by how well we say things but how well we are understood.

Andrew Grove

I t's relatively easy to manage systems, but infinitely more complicated to lead people. That's why great leaders are great communicators. To manage a system, you just need to provide inputs, outputs,
and processes. To lead people, you have to inform, question, listen,
receive feedback, offer clarifications, ensure understanding, and maintain a common purpose.

Talking is easy. Providing information is easy. Communication is hard. There's a big difference between conversation, information, and communication. Talking is a social activity and
information is based on facts. You talk to and inform people to let
them know what's going on, but you communicate to provide
much, much more. You communicate to reduce conflict, build connections, establish relationships, earn trust, demonstrate integrity,
prevent misunderstandings, improve morale, motivate performance,
and ultimately build a following.

Above all, though, leadership communication is made up of
efforts to unify a team, their purpose, and their understanding.
Whether you're making efforts to choose the right direction, align

work with goals, or build influence with others, your efforts to under-stand or be understood will determine your effectiveness. The better you communicate, the more likely your directions will make sense, your teammates will understand their work, and everyone will want to follow you. You just have to remember that leadership communication is not based on what you are saying. It's based on what everyone else understands.

It's much like the approach I take toward teaching. My philosophy has always been, "It doesn't matter how well you are teaching. It only matters how well your students are learning." As a communicator, I try to take the same approach. It doesn't matter what you are saying. It only matters what everyone else is understanding. You have to connect with your audience before your message will be effective. The better you know the individuals with whom you are sharing that message, the better you can present the information in a manner they can follow.

Everyone learns a bit differently because everyone is wired to think a bit differently. According to psychologist and author Howard Gardner, there are eight forms of intelligence (or eight forms of learning). They are language, logical/mathematical, spatial, musical, kinesthetic (action), naturalistic, interpersonal, and intrapersonal. If you only appeal to one form of intelligence by communicating with everyone the same way, you'll be leaving a lot of people behind. There is a big difference between delivering the perfect message and perfectly delivering a message. With the former, you say the right things. With the latter, people leave knowing what those things are.

Next Level: Engage the Village

Next-level communicators don't just work on how they communicate, though. They go the extra step of creating a culture of team communication. The greatest teams don't just understand their work; they understand each other and each other's work. When teammates understand everyone else and what they do, they can help the team grow. Without that understanding, it's nearly impossible to add value to each other's lives.

To add that value, teammates must be able to share thoughts, experiences, and opinions. Creating a culture of communication is really about building a culture of trust. People have to know they can be honest without fear of repercussions and speak their mind without ridicule. It's the only way everyone can use their collective knowledge, opinions, and wisdom to add value to one another's work and one another's lives. Knowledge, insight, and wisdom are only valuable to the team if they are shared, and no one will share their thoughts if that type of feedback isn't embraced and encouraged.

I think a major portion of quality leadership communication comes down to how well everyone on the team gives and receives feedback. Feedback is specifically meant to provide someone with the information they need to improve some aspect of their plans or performance. From that perspective, feedback should be welcomed and free flowing. That type of culture requires two things: an open mind and an open mouth. If everyone has the confidence to share some hard truths and everyone is willing to accept them as a means of improving performance, there's no limit to what they can accomplish.

Yes, I know. That type of feedback is usually called criticism, but most people don't like to be criticized. Some leaders try to soften the blow by calling it constructive criticism, but any type of criticism is usually used to point out the negative aspects of someone's performance. I like using the term constructive *feedback* because the goal is to improve, not just point out flaws. When you criticize, you focus on negative behaviors in the past. When you constructively offer feedback, you focus on developing stronger behaviors for the future. Consultants Eric Harvey and Alexander Lucia agree, and advise using the TIPS model for giving feedback to others. They teach the following principles to help teams and individuals harness the power of feedback:

Timely: Always provide constructive feedback as soon as possible. When time passes, we may forget the details that make the biggest difference.

Individualized: People don't make improvements based on broad, general feedback given to a large group. It has to be personal before it will be beneficial. Otherwise, everyone just assumes you're talking to someone else.

Productive: Make the most of the time you have together by saying what needs to be said and keeping the focus on improvement. Anything else is a waste of time.

Specific: If we want employees to improve in specific areas, we have to give specific feedback. Telling someone to sell your products better will not increase sales. Coaching them on the company's customer service policy and modeling proper sales strategies will.

This type of culture is not easy to build, but it can be done. The trick is that it starts with your willingness to give and receive feedback. If everyone knows that you will be open to their honest opinion, they will be much more likely to give it. When you create a culture where information can be shared freely and without judgment, you're really building a culture that allows you to make better decisions, build stronger relationships, and ensure the alignment between what is being done and what should be done.

Where We Go Wrong

We don't listen.

Listening opens doors to all kinds of possibilities. It's the most important aspect of communication. Nothing that has been said has ever really made a difference in this world. It's what has been heard, understood, and accepted that has made the difference. I always try to follow the advice of my friend Chris Daniel, who told me, "If you want to be the best prepared person in any situation, always make every effort to dominate the listening." I love that phrase! Think of what you could learn by setting a goal to dominate the listening in any conversation.

To truly listen, it's about being engaged with the person who is speaking and building a desire to hear what they have to say. It's the only way to understand them. Discussions are not competitions, but we often view them as such. When others are talking, many people only listen because they're waiting on their chance to speak. That's called competitive listening, and it stems from a desire to be heard and a need to be right. If we can eliminate those needs and replace them with a desire to hear and understand, we would strengthen every relationship we have.

Listening isn't just about collecting information, though. It's also about letting other people know that you've heard them. When you cut people off or shut them down you may miss a chance to connect with them. Coach Rick Pitino said he learned the value of this connection when he was recruiting college basketball players. He and his assistants had always tried to use the short time they had with a recruit and his family to outline every positive aspect of their program. They felt their only chance to get the player was to sell him and his family on the benefits of their team. What he found was that the opposite was really true. When he listened to the needs and fears of the family, he was able to build a much stronger connection with them and ultimately landed more recruits.

When talking to someone, poor communicators focus more on what they're going to say next than they do on what the other person is saying. To listen, it means you withhold your reaction until you've heard what someone else has said. If you have something to say, find the appropriate moment to say it, not just the first moment available. Listening is more than just a great communication skill. It's a great people skill. When you speak, you're telling someone what you consider to be important. When you listen, you're letting someone know that you consider <u>them</u> to be important. Who doesn't want to know that?

We take understanding for granted.

One of the worst communication mistakes a leader can make is to assume their team has developed the same understanding of a message, process, or direction as he or she has developed. In reality, unless you have made very intentional efforts to make sure everyone is on the same page, they're probably not. Everyone operates in different worlds with different experiences and different perspectives, yet many times a message is only delivered one way and the leader expects everyone to grasp it.

The need for understanding is greater now more than ever. Not too long ago an order given by a boss would not be questioned, whether it was understood or not. Today, it's an expectation that orders will be accompanied by an explanation. If an explanation isn't given or it makes no sense, it's often assumed that the order isn't worth following. A lot of leaders don't like the new reality and choose to ignore it, but ignoring reality doesn't make it any less real.

Regardless of their motivations, however, most people just have a natural desire to understand. It's how they frame reality. If the leader doesn't provide that understanding, people will insert their own. The trouble is, many times that new reality isn't real, at all. Misunderstandings are powerful barriers to the alignment of work and goals, and with today's social media technology misinformation can spread to thousands of employees in seconds. Misperception is like a forest fire. Catch it early and you can put it out with your foot. Ignore it and you'll have to call in the National Guard.

Information is sought, but never shared.

I've seen way too many leaders adopt a "power position" when it comes to communication. They want to use knowledge as a means of increasing their own importance or building political alliances by only sharing information when it benefits them. Great teams aren't built by using or withholding information. They are built by sharing it so everyone knows exactly what's going on. It's a powerful concept, and one that nearly changed the outcome of World War II.

The Manhattan Project was the U. S. government's initiative to develop the first atomic bomb. The mission was kept such a secret that even the team members didn't know why they were working on their individual assignments. Because of the secrecy, the pieces weren't coming together. It was looking as though the initiative was going to fail until J. Robert Oppenheimer was selected to take over the project. He brought the people together to explain what they were doing and why they were doing it. He wanted to make sure that everyone knew their work was more than just an experimental project. He wanted them to know that their efforts may very well determine the fate of the free world.

Oppenheimer was not the logical choice to lead the development of the atom bomb. He had no administrative experience, studied a different type of physics, and not many people really liked him. In the end, however, he succeeded brilliantly because he made sure every department and every individual understood both the vision and their contribution. Information was shared freely and every member of the lab felt they could contribute to something worthwhile. Because of that new level of communication, the mission was a success and the rest, as they say, is history.

How to Communicate Better

Work on your Communication SKILLS.

It's vitally important to deliver a clear message so the team understands how to navigate the processes that lead to the accomplishment of their goals. If you want to make sure you're making the most out of your time and effort communicating with your team, work on your Communication SKILLS:

Seek information.

Keep an open mind.

Invite feedback and opinions.

Learn all you can.

Listen to what people mean.

Speak openly and honestly.

Adhering to those guidelines will help you choose the right directions, but more importantly they will help you influence others to unite and follow you. Notice that five of the six SKILLS apply to the way you gather and absorb information, and only one pertains to the way you provide it. The only way to improve the quality of the message you deliver is to improve the quality of what you understand.

When you seek information, you do more than just improve what you know, though. It's not just about building your knowledge base, but telling everyone else that you value what they have to offer. It's a good feeling for teammates when you openly invite their feedback. If you do, it will improve every aspect of your ability to lead because your message will be accurate and your team will feel a stronger connection with it.

In the end, once you have determined what needs to be done and are ready to deliver that message, the most important thing is to speak openly and honestly. Information is only useful when it's complete and accurate, and honest information will be both.

Think before you speak.

Momma said it best: "Think before you speak." That simple little strategy would save a lot of relationships and a lot of jobs. You can't always determine what happens around you, but you can always choose your response to it. The more you think about that response, the greater your chance of acting and reacting appropriately.

Have you ever heard some of the following types of phrases used to describe someone's negative behavior? "Jim really flew off the handle yesterday." "Sara came unglued when she heard what happened in production." "Robert lost it in the meeting this morning." These are things people say when someone has acted in a way that doesn't reflect positive behavior. They also describe people who have acted before they thought about what they should do.

Coach Urban Meyer, the highly successful head football coach of The Ohio State University, certainly believes in the power of responses. He teaches the following as a guiding principle for success: $E + R = O$. It stands for Event plus Response equals Outcome. He says, "You can't always control the event, but what you can control is your response." Through this philosophy he wants his players to understand that ultimately they control their outcomes by controlling what they think and what they do.

The same is true for us. Leaders who make the most of their responses will have a much easier time getting the most from their outcomes. Leaders who make the most of their ability to think will be much more likely to make the most of those responses.

Stick to the point.

Communication must be organized to be effective. Rambling speeches and scattered presentations do nothing to help people understand and remember the most important things. If you want to set priorities and unify direction, you need to have a main point, then support that point. Too many times I've seen speakers and leaders have several "main" points. When this happens, everyone in the room goes away with a different understanding of the most important priorities.

My friend David Loving, who has run several hospitals throughout the Southeastern United States, told me I could learn all I needed to know about effective communication in sixth-grade English class. He said every elementary school student learns how to write a topic sentence and use the rest of the paragraph to support that opening statement. Great communicators follow the same pattern when they deliver a message. They let everyone know why they're speaking then use the rest of their time to support that topic.

To ensure that you stick to the point, I am a huge advocate of the KISS method: Keep It Short and Simple. People aren't going to remember everything you tell them. If you want them to remember the things that truly matter, make those things the bulk of your message. If you try to make too many points people will only remember various parts of the message. You'll just be leaving it up to chance as to whether or not they'll remember the important ones.

Learn to communicate electronically.

A great deal of our communication today is done in an electronic format. There are a lot of positive aspects of electronic communication (or e-comm), but only when used properly. E-comm is like salt. Use the right amount, and it'll enhance your message. Use too much, and you'll leave everyone with a bad taste in their mouth.

You can't rely too heavily on e-mail and other media to serve as your main method of communicating. E-comm should be an extension of the personal contact, not a replacement. You can share information across a computer screen, but you can't connect with people, foster relationships, motivate performance, build trust, earn respect, or gain influence. Those things require a personal touch.

When used properly, though, electronic communication is a wonderful tool to have at your disposal. Just remember that when you send an electronic message, it's permanent. If you make grammatical errors or a mistake in the content, you appear as though you are either incompetent about the subject or just plain incompetent. Neither one is a good thing for a leader trying to build influence with her or his team. If you want to improve the quality of your e-comm skills, use the following rules as a guide:

Eight Effective E-comm Essentials

- Proofread each message. It only takes a minute, and every mistake you find is credibility you didn't lose.

- Don't send a message to ten people if you're only talking to two.

- Never send personal information in a mass email. If you have a car for sale or a puppy that needs a good home, the workplace email system is not the place to advertise.

- Don't use all caps unless you intend to yell.

- Sarcasm does not read well in print. The purpose of sarcasm is to say one thing and mean another. Without facial expressions and body language, you say one thing and mean that thing.

- Have someone else read something harsh or controversial before you send it.

- If you want your message to be read, be brief.

- If you want your message to be understood, be clear.

To Summarize, Next-Level Communication Is...

...understanding.

When I started college, the first three people with whom I spoke kept telling me about the importance of general education courses and how certain credit hours related to my academic plan. When I asked someone for clarification, they kindly explained to me the concepts of general education courses and my academic plan. I nodded and they went on to talk about something else, but I was still confused. You see, it wasn't general education or an academic plan that had me puzzled. I had no idea what a credit hour was. Without that basic knowledge, there was no way I could understand the rest of the message.

Remember, the Leadership Point-of-View is looking at the world through the eyes of others, so the most important thing is not what you say, but what everyone else understands. Speaking well is never enough for proper leadership communication. Speaking well just means that you understand what you're talking about. You have to relate to people so they can understand what you're talking about.

You have to make connections with their experiences so they understand the message. If you don't, you'll be like the misguided teacher who said, "I know it and I taught it; my students just didn't learn it." Your effectiveness as a teacher is not measured by what you know. It's measured by what your students know. It's the same with leadership. Your success doesn't depend on what you know and say. Your success depends on what your team hears and understands.

Many teachers will use the Whole-Part-Whole method to help ensure understanding. They will first outline the big picture, and then break it into smaller, more easily understood components. Through-out the process they will periodically show their students the whole picture again to make sure those students know how the smaller parts work to accomplish the overall objective. This is one of the best methods I know to ensure understanding because it gives people the context of the situation, then the information they need in order to make a contribution. When people only know what they have to do, but have no idea why they're doing it, it's really hard for them to find their purpose and connect with their work.

Too many times, however, we take a simple concept and make it complicated by adding too much information or using confusing language. Consider the following passage:

Two youths traversed an inclined plan, seeking the procurement of a quantity of a potable liquid. One youth had an unexpectedly rapid decent and suffered multiple lacerations, contusions, and a fractured cranium whilst the second youth followed a similar trajectory.

Did you recognize that as the story of Jack and Jill who went up the hill to fetch a pail of water? The content of the message correctly related the story, but it wasn't nearly as easy to understand as the storybook version.

The greatest communicators have the ability to take something complicated and make it very simple. To do this, you just have to focus on clarity, not quantity. When your focus is clarity you highlight the most important things as simply as you possibly can so people will understand your message. When you focus on quantity you don't highlight anything in an effort to touch on everything and people remember nothing.

Great leaders are great because they elevate people above what they could have done on their own. They choose great directions, align their team's actions with those directions, and influence people to achieve their goals. Without the ability to help others align their work with success and inspire them to follow you in that direction, you'll just go there by yourself; and you certainly won't add value to their life. Quite simply, if you can't communicate, you can't elevate.

The Five Commandments of Communication

Thou shalt listen with a passion.

Thou shalt know thy audience.

Thou shalt know thy purpose.

Thou shalt stick to thy purpose.

Thou shalt ensure understanding.

Next-Level Change-Leadership

When the rate of change on the inside of an institution becomes slower than the rate of change on the outside, the end is in sight.

Jack Welch

hange is very important to our lives. Any time we seek growth or strive for something better, we're basically saying we want something different than what we currently have. If you want to make that happen, you either have to make changes to where you are or what you do. You can't stay in the same place and do the same things and expect to have better results.

I've seen the term "change-management" for many years and even used it for the first part of my career. After many years leading change, though, I've come to realize that change isn't effective when it's managed. Change is only effective when it's led. True change doesn't occur as a result of a process or a plan. True change only occurs within the hearts, minds, and behaviors of people. That's why I now refer to the process of leading change as change-*leadership*, not change-*management*. It places the importance on the people.

All my life I have heard that people don't respond well to change. To be honest, I have a hard time believing that. In fact, history tells a completely different story. From the discovery of new lands and the industrialization of economies to manned space travel and the information age, we have changed a great deal over the last two hundred years. Heck, we've changed a lot over the last ten years! If people didn't do well with change, we'd be writing letters by candlelight and riding horses to work.

People will change. We just have to be aware that they don't accept it based on our understanding. They accept it based on their understanding, and their resulting perception. It's that perception of the change and its necessity that truly matters. A few years ago I had lunch with our state demographer, Ron Crouch, and he asked me, "Juston, do you know the difference between perception and reality?" Before I could answer he said, "The difference is that reality changes. People's perceptions rarely do."

Of course, his point was that a failure to change our perception of the world often puts us at odds with reality. That's why change has to occur on a personal level, not an organizational level. Leaders who lead change with a procedure focus rather than a people focus are missing the most important aspect of change-leadership. Changing a procedure has no effect on the results. You have to change what people know and what people do in order to have an impact.

Change at a personal level is really about breaking old habits and starting new ones, and habits are hard to break, my friends. As leaders, though, we have a duty to lead the process of change when those old habits no longer align with success. Once it becomes clear that something has to change, it's the leader's responsibility to find a new direction, help the team understand it, align their work with that direction, and influence them to follow.

Teams who resist change are really resisting their chance to excel. When we avoid change, what we're really avoiding is growth. Anne

Mulcahy faced this reality when she became the CEO of Xerox in 2001. She inherited a corporation that had grown complacent and irrelevant after several years of strong performance. While Xerox had built a strong business for the 1980s-era market, their failure to change with the times led to outdated practices and a sluggish response to the new technology-based market of the 1990s. Mulcahy knew the only thing that would save the company was change.

She traveled the country and met with hundreds and hundreds of people until she felt like she knew what needed to be done. She took that feedback and initiated changes to make Xerox more cost efficient and relevant. She streamlined the workforce, cut expenditures, sold various pieces of the corporation, and invested in research and development. As a result of those change efforts, the company became more technology based and its stock price climbed each year while she was the CEO.

Still, it wasn't easy. Some of the actions she had to take were very painful, but a failure to make those changes would have hurt even worse. Her philosophy was, "Companies disappear because they can't reinvent themselves." Well, Xerox reinvented itself and became relevant to a paperless society, but the people involved had to make some serious adjustments. I mean, think about the change-leadership it required to take over the largest plain paper copying business in the world and set a goal of eliminating paper within ten years!

All-in-all, change is the only way to win in today's fast-paced world. Globalization, technology, and increased competition for customers have mandated that every organization has to do more with less, continually update their processes, retool their equipment, and retrain their people. The only way to stay viable as an organization is to keep growing. The only way to keep growing is to keep changing.

Next Level: Staying Ahead

We take change-leadership to the next level by using it to keep ahead instead of just using it to keep up. The old maxim "If it ain't broke don't fix it" can be problematic. Most people tend to change only when it's necessary. That approach, however, means that we only change after it becomes clear that we should. At that point, an opportunity has already passed or a service has already become obsolete. It's why Apple introduces a new iPhone long before the old one has run its course. The leaders at Apple know they can't lead change by waiting for something else to drive it.

While I do believe you don't just change for change's sake, I would personally not want to wait until my product or service is irrelevant to go about trying to "fix" it. It's the same reason I don't wait until the engine locks up in my car to change the oil. By taking the don't-fix-it-unless-it's-broken philosophy, you only change after a problem has occurred. I would rather be a little more proactive than that.

Unfortunately, the reality is that most teams and organizations don't start looking at change until it becomes necessary. Of course, what this really means is that the *leader* doesn't start looking at change until it becomes necessary. Trouble is, at that point you're talking about change from a position of weakness. My friend Peter Feil, Vice President of Stober Drives International, once told me that he always strives to change from a position of strength. In his words, "When you change before you have to, you have control. You stand a much better chance of succeeding if the company is driving the actions of change, not letting change drive the actions of the company."

Where We Go Wrong

Lack of communication.

When we think of the support needed to help others change, we often think of training or resources, but no support is more important than communication. It's the only way your team can understand what they need to do and why they need to do it. At its most basic level, change-leadership can be broken into three phases: before, during, and after. At each of those stages, it will be the team's understanding that determines your success.

Before a change is made, we have to make sure that the direction we have chosen makes sense. Leaders must gather mounds of data and loads of feedback. Making a change is a very big deal. Every change-leader has a duty to make sure it's going to be in everyone's best interest. It's the information you collect beforehand that will determine how likely you will be to make the right call.

Of course, after you make that call, you have to get started. When people are working toward the new and unknown, the "unknown" portion doesn't just make change scary; it makes change difficult. The more you communicate with your teammates while implementing the change, the more reassurance and guidance you can provide. A steady flow of information is needed to build momentum and assure actions are aligned with the new direction. If you give people a chance to ask questions and provide feedback, it gives them security, and it gives you a chance to make sure people are on the right track. The worst thing that can happen is for the wheels to be falling off and you don't even know it. It'll lead to current failure and future resistance.

Communication can't stop after implementation, though. After the change has been made, you have to make sure people understand how things are going. If you want performance to continue in the new direction, people have to know that it's working. If they lack that information, they may be tempted to fall back into old habits and old comfort zones after just a few months.

Change is forced.

Have you ever noticed that change is never resisted by the people driving it? Those people are informed and invested. It's resisted by the ones who haven't spent time developing an understanding of it. This may seem glaringly obvious from afar, but when you're the one initiating a change, it can be easy to forget that everyone else may not see the benefits as clearly as you do. It's easy to lose sight of the fact that everyone else is perfectly happy doing what they're currently doing and may not find value in changing course.

This is the trap into which a lot of leaders fall. They see beyond the shadow of a doubt that the change will be beneficial for the team but never take the time to help the employees see it for themselves. When you see that it's time to make a change, you have to make sure others have a chance to gain the same perspective. If they don't understand the benefits of what you're asking them to do, you'll be mandating action instead of leading action.

The leader resists the change.

We often talk about how the team or a few employees resist change, but I've seen just as many cases where the leader was the one resisting a new direction. I don't know how many times I've seen leaders fail because they do nothing to step up and lead a new initiative even when they know a change is needed. Always remember that facts are facts. Ignoring them doesn't make them go away. When the facts indicate that we could or should do something differently, we have a responsibility to make a change. The more honestly we confront the realities, the easier it is to accept the change.

MIT professor James Utterback did some research and found many examples of companies who became totally irrelevant just because they were unwilling to embrace changes in the environment. One of the examples he uses is the highly successful ice-shipping industries of the 19th century. At that time, packing and shipping ice was a very lucrative business. It was the only way to refrigerate food south of the frozen North. Anyone with an ice box had to have ice. Yet most of those packing and shipping plants refused to recognize the change brought about by the invention of home ice-making machines. Because of this, rather than making a change that would keep them relevant, those companies lost everything. Of course, it wasn't the companies resisting the change. It was the leaders.

How to Become a Better Change-Leader

Use the Trinity of Understanding.

Most people don't resist change because they hate change; they resist it because they don't know why it's necessary or why it would be in their best interest. People have to understand what they're being asked to do and why they're being asked to do it before they will truly embrace a new direction. I believe the best way to establish this type of understanding is a threefold process. Individuals have to understand why the current situation isn't working, why the proposed change will be better, and what it means for them. I call this The Trinity of Understanding.

The Trinity of Understanding

Understand Why the Change Is Necessary

Understand Why the Change Will Be Better

Understand What It Means to the Individual

One of the most overlooked aspects of any effort to lead change is an explanation of why the current situation isn't working or why it won't work in the future. More times than not, leaders jump straight to an explanation of why a change will be better. If people still believe the path they're on is perfectly fine, though, it's hard to convince them to go another way. It's really a valid point. I mean, why would anyone want to leave their comfort zone if they think it's working just fine? When people don't know why they need to change, they'll have a hard time finding value in doing something different.

Once folks understand there is a justified reason to change course you can start helping them understand why the new direction will be beneficial. At that point, if you can help them envision a better future, they will be more likely to embrace that future and the work involved in getting there. People may change what they do because they are *told* to do something new, but they will only change what they value when they *want* to do something new. When people learn enough about a new direction to value it, change truly gains momentum.

Just remember that you can't stop there, though. Understanding why the change is better still doesn't necessarily mean someone has a desire to get on board. If one of your teammates has no idea what it means for them, they still may resist the unknown because they may fear what it means on a personal level. If you don't address what the change means for the individual, you'll never alleviate their fear of becoming irrelevant. Once everyone understands that the new direction will be good for the company and that they will be able to contribute, they will have a much easier time embracing the new realities.

The Trinity of Understanding also provides a great system of checks and balances. If you can't fully explain why the change is necessary, perhaps you don't need to change. If you can't fully explain why the change will be better, perhaps you need to look in another direction. If you can't fully explain what the change means for the employee, perhaps you don't know enough about it to implement it. In any case, utilizing the Trinity of Understanding will give you a much greater chance of making your change-leadership efforts work for everyone.

Follow the Trinity of Support.

In the end, though, it's not just about making the change. It's about making the change work. As an extension of the Trinity of Understanding, we have to be mindful that to be effective, change must be long-lasting. Because of this, we should also consider the Trinity of Support.

The Trinity of Support

Support for the Change

Support for the Individual

Support for the Implementation

The Trinity of Understanding builds desire, but it takes continuing support to build a new comfort zone. If employees have the desire to change but don't possess the resources or skills to succeed in the new direction, they will most likely prefer to see the change fail so they can get back to the old ways. To fully support the change, you want to make it as easy as you can for your team to make it work. To give everyone the best chance for long-lasting success, you need to provide support to make the change process possible, support for the individuals to do the work, and support for its overall implementation.

The process should always begin with support for the change. The most important aspects are providing resources and setting clear expectations. The infrastructure and resources must be appropriate and available before you can expect any change to work. You have to ensure that even the most basic needs are in place. For instance, I've seen several software changes fail because no one took the time to ensure the compatibility of the company's equipment. Without the proper resources, you're just setting yourself up for change-failure right from the start.

Likewise, one of the most important (and often overlooked) aspects of supporting a change is to make sure that people clearly understand what's expected. The first step is to define what success looks like and how it will be measured. When people don't understand the new goals, they have no idea how to connect with them. Without that clarity, people will invent their own realities, and you'll have change going in twenty different directions.

Just remember that you also have to support the people who are making the change. Too many times teams lose momentum because all the attention is focused on the process, not the people. In all reality, it's not a procedure you're changing. It's behavior. People need opportunities to develop the skills that will keep them relevant. By offering that type of training you not only develop your workforce but give them peace of mind about the new direction.

Finally, to make change long-lasting and effective, its implementation must be supported long enough to become the new comfort zone. If it's not, there is always the danger that your teammates will fall back into old habits. You have to stay with the change project throughout its entirety. As the leader, you can't walk away just because a process has been implemented. You have to remain involved until you're sure everyone else is convinced it's the right way to go. It's inevitable that problems will arise, and unless you help everyone work through them, you may lose your momentum. It takes time to prove that a new direction will pay off, and it's very often during this time that teams fall back into their old ways. If you can provide proof that the change has worked, however, you can create a new comfort zone. Until then, you're only providing an alternative to what they already know and love.

Basically, Next-Level Change Is...

...culture.

Change shouldn't be seen as isolated incidents. In order for you, your team, and your organization to make the most out of change, it has to be more than just a project. It has to become a culture. If the culture exists to embrace change, you don't have to worry about getting people on board. You just have to worry about choosing the right direction and supporting your teammates' efforts to make it work. However, you don't build culture overnight. You have to build positive momentum over time.

When I first started teaching, I was encouraged to watch a movie called *Stand and Deliver*. It told the story of a math teacher named Jaime Escalante who was hired to teach at Garfield High School in East Los Angeles. My principal wanted me to see the film so I would be inspired to make a difference in my students' lives, and while it was a very inspirational story, I think it taught me much more about the value of momentum when leading change.

Garfield was one of the worst schools in the nation and was in danger of receiving sanctions on their accreditation as a public school, which would pretty much ruin what little chance the students had for a quality education. Escalante decided he would try to start an AP Calculus program as an attempt to give the best students at Garfield a chance to succeed in life. It was a pretty big change to implement for a school whose students barely passed any test, much less an AP test. In the first year of the program, he had no momentum and battled a culture of underachievement.

He scraped up enough students to start the class, but after just a couple of weeks had already lost half of them. When it was time to take the AP test, only five students remained, and only two passed. Still, it was a start. Two was better than zero.

The next year he started with nine students. Eight finished the course and six of them passed the exam. Escalante was gaining momentum. The following year, he began with 15 students. All of them finished the course and 14 passed the AP test. By the fall of 1981, he began with 18 students, and again 14 passed the exam. This time, though, there was a problem.

An official grading the exams accused Escalante and his students of cheating. It was an easy accusation to make. I mean, how could students from such a low-achieving school be passing one of the toughest exams in the nation? Those officials decided that all of the students would have to retake the test under the scrutiny of an evaluator. It was the only way to justify their success.

In the end, every student passed the second test. At this point, the momentum was unstoppable. Confidence and support was at an all-time high and the culture had changed at Garfield High School. In the fall of 1983, 31 students enrolled in the AP calculus program. The next year, 63 signed up. By 1987, 129 students took the AP exam and an incredible 85 of them passed.

If you want to make change easier for the people you lead, you have to create momentum for the new direction. When you do, people will see that others are successful and will have an easier time making the transition. In fact, they will want to do it. Building momentum actually means that you are building a culture of success, and who doesn't want to be a part of that?

Next-Level Implementation

*Some people want it to happen, some wish it would happen,
and others make it happen.*

Michael Jordan

For anything we do, the past, present, and future are all important. We think about what happened yesterday so can we learn from the past, and we look to the future to see where we want to be. What truly makes us successful, though, is the work we do today. Yesterday is gone and tomorrow hasn't happened. Today is the only time in which we can truly make a difference. Next-Level Implementation is all about making today count so that we have a better tomorrow.

It's easy to get caught up in the future because it contains what we want. As a result, I believe too many people become goal-oriented. Goals are very important, but they don't achieve themselves. That's why I value being goal-driven, but *process*-oriented. When you spend the majority of your time thinking about goals you may be motivated to accomplish what you set out to do, but find it hard to focus on the steps that get you there. If you can train yourself to be process-oriented, however, you will devote your day-to-day energy to the things that will actually lead to reaching your objectives.

Goals and results are attractive, though, because they are out there for everyone to see. We just have to constantly remind ourselves that those are not the aspects of the team's work that deserve the most attention. It's what goes on beneath the surface that truly matters. If you think of leadership and achievement as an iceberg, you can see that goals and results are visible only because so much is being done below the surface to keep them afloat. Leaders and teams who give the majority of their attention to goals and results would ignore the most important aspects of achieving them.

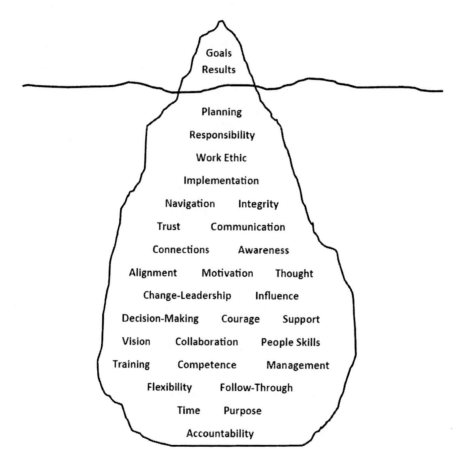

I believe that Newton's third law of motion, "for every action there is an equal and opposite reaction," applies to life as much as it does to physics. If you want big success, you have to give big effort. It takes a lot of work and a lot of time to achieve significant goals. The catch is, we don't do big things each day. We do big things by continuously making the most out of the little things each day.

Leadership is action. More precisely, leadership is the coordination of action in the right direction. Leaders are responsible for casting visions, but more importantly, they are responsible for making those visions become reality. Every one of us is ultimately judged by our results, and results only come when the right work gets done.

Much of the success or failure you experience during implementation will be determined by your approach to the process. You need an implementation plan to include all of the elements it takes to go from design to evaluation. A good general model is what I call the PINE Model. PINE stands for Planning, Implementation, Navigation, and Evaluation. While it certainly doesn't address all the finer points of the work you'll need to do, it does provide a good overall philosophy to frame your leadership during the implementation of any initiative.

PINE Model

Planning: The better you plan the work of your team, the greater the potential that their work will make a difference. If work isn't planned well, it likely won't be done well.

Implementation: Getting a job done can't happen until you get it started.

Navigation: Great leaders must be able to change course when necessary. Problems are going to pop up. You have to be willing to adjust in order to progress.

Evaluation: When a job is done, it's extremely important to take time to evaluate what went well and what did not. You never want to repeat mistakes from the past or fail to repeat successes in the future.

The process of implementation is really where the rubber meets the road for your efforts to lead. I believe in goals, dreams, and ideas, but also believe they only account for 10% of the formula for success. The other 90% is what we are willing to do about them. Implementation is what truly matters when we talk about making a difference in the world, our work, or our personal lives. If you want to add value to your organization or your teammates, it has to be produced, not dreamt.

Taking It to the Next Level: Providing Support

Doing the work it takes to implement any process requires a good deal of support. As leaders, that's really our most important role in the implementation process. Our teammates need support, and they need to know they have it. Support is important for two reasons: (a) it helps people do their work and (b) it helps them feel more confident they'll reach their goals. It's much easier to do good work when it's supported from the leader, and all-in-all it's just a good feeling to know someone has your back.

On the other hand, the absence of support can stifle the work and cause a great deal of harm to the leader/follower relationship. When reading The United States of America's *Declaration of Independence*, you will see that the Founding Fathers developed a list of grievances against England and King George to justify a separation from British rule. Those grievances included the unwelcome presence of a military force, unfair taxes, unjust punishments, and acts of violence committed against the Colonies. Despite the severity of those complaints, however, many of them dealt with the King's lack of support for the work of the colonists. Review the first five grievances below:

- He (King George) has refused his Assent to the Laws most necessary for the public good.

- He has forbidden his Governors to pass Laws of immediate and pressing importance; and when so suspended, he has utterly neglected to attend to them.

- He has refused to pass other Laws for the accommodation of large districts of People, unless those People would relinquish the right of Representation in the legislature.

- He has called together legislative bodies at places unusual, uncomfortable, and distant from the depository of their Public Records, for the sole purpose of fatiguing them into compliance with his measures.

- He has dissolved Representative Houses repeatedly for opposing his invasions on the rights of the People.

The Colonists had become so frustrated with the lack of support and understanding they were receiving from their leader that they decided war was a better alternative. Hopefully we'll never find ourselves in a situation where a lack of support would result in war, but the sentiment is the same. If you want your teammates to feel good about working hard for you, they have to believe you are equally willing to work hard for them.

As next-level leaders we have to move beyond what it takes for us to succeed, and focus on what it takes for our teammates to succeed. It will be the investments we make in them that will determine our results. When you help your teammates grow, you give them the tools they need to succeed in the present and prepare for the future. The greatest support a leader can give is to make sure today's effort is making progress toward tomorrow's success.

Where We Go Wrong

We don't prioritize our time and attention.

Establishing priorities is critical to the implementation process. Everything cannot be the most important thing, and everything cannot get equal attention. If your car has a leak in the brake line and a broken radio, you'd better make the brake line a greater priority. A Navy Admiral once advised a rising officer, "Your job is to figure out what's important, and act on it. Period." That's some really good advice for aspiring leaders. If you want to accomplish your most important goals, you have to spend your time doing the most important work.

Prioritization really comes down to two factors: knowing your goals and dedicating the majority of your time toward the work that gets them done. You can't focus on the first thing that comes your way, and you can't focus on everything that comes your way. You have to focus on the most important things. Period.

We fail to engage everyone in their work.

The implementation process is much easier for everyone if you can find ways to keep people engaged in what they do. If you want people to connect with their day-to-day duties, they have to know why they're doing the work and they have to know why it matters. Goals such as hitting $1,000,000 in sales or an annual customer satisfaction rating of 98% are only numbers – and numbers aren't engaging. It's the work that must be engaging, not the goal. If the work has meaning, the goal will become a natural result.

If your teammates are not engaged in their work, they will likely not do it very well. For example, I've often heard stories about how our service men and women hate the physical training, or PT, they must constantly endure. First Lieutenant Buddy Gengler's unit was no different. That is, until the day they almost got Lt. Gengler killed.

During a ground mission in Iraq, the men were dropped farther than expected from a target facility, and they had to make a run for it. Gengler, being in great physical condition, arrived at the hot zone about 60 yards ahead of his men. This meant that he was alone, without cover, for many seconds (an eternity in a firefight, I'm told). After that mission, his soldiers scheduled PT the very next day and went to work. PT suddenly became more than just something the bosses always made them do. It was connected to something much more meaningful.

Once that connection is made, we just need to help people stay motivated to keep pushing toward their goals. While there are hundreds of motivational strategies, the best one I know is encouragement. An ounce of encouragement is better than a pound of fear to keep people engaged in their work. That's why I like to provide Intrusive Encouragement. I try to find something of value to praise every day. I've found that the more time I spend praising the good behavior, the less time I have to spend punishing the bad behavior. You are more apt to keep positive action by praising it than you are to eliminate negative action by punishing it. You'll find that what you celebrate, you replicate.

We try to do it all (we don't delegate).

Any time you come into a position of authority, you are expected to spend your time a little differently than you did as a follower. Leaders are hired to handle the big issues, not the small ones. A university president once told me, "Here's what I do when trying to decide which duties to delegate: If someone else can do the job, I delegate it. I'm supposed to spend my time doing the work no one else can do."

There's a lot of merit to that philosophy. When leaders spend their time doing the work that no one else can do, it means the team will be in a position to do more than it did before the leader got there. If the leader spends her or his time doing work that someone else could do, what difference would it make?

You just have to remember that while delegation helps you maximize team effort by distributing work, the work will always be your responsibility. That's why you can't delegate and walk away. You have to maintain contact to make sure people have what they need to get the job done and that the job being done is the right one. Just don't confuse staying in contact with staying in control. Don't delegate an assignment if you intend to micromanage it yourself. To help frame your approach to delegation, consider the following:

Dos and Don'ts of Delegation

<u>Do</u>	<u>Don't</u>
Monitor progress	Micromanage details
Provide feedback	Leave them guessing
Share accountability	Blame others for failure
Recognize a job well done	Take credit when the project is over
Give support	Meddle
Trust people to do the work	Walk away and never look back

Empowering your people through delegation means you have the opportunity to let others shine and perhaps even find some hidden talents. Many times a low-ranking position keeps your best leaders from leading. When you create opportunities for those people to chair committees or take on special projects, you not only get some important work done but you give them a chance to develop skills that will prepare them to lead their own teams. That type of growth will pay dividends for years to come.

How to Improve Your Implementation Skills

Provide structure.

You need more than just a work ethic to be highly successful. You need a <u>disciplined</u> work ethic so your short-term effort will have the greatest long-term effect. It's why great teams and great people don't shy away from discipline. In fact, they want it. They know in their hearts that there is an undeniable link between discipline and success.

I once heard a story at a coaching clinic that explained the true benefit of discipline. It was about two dog owners who had different philosophies of discipline. The first owner believed that puppies needed a great deal of structure. He constantly corrected the dog, spanked it with a newspaper when it did something wrong, told it "no" repeatedly, and only rewarded her when she earned the treat. The second owner wanted the cute little puppy to be happy, so he just let it do whatever it wanted and provided treats for no reason at all. He couldn't believe anyone would treat a pet with such harsh discipline as the first owner.

Two years later, both dog owners were in the city park. The first dog was very well-behaved and had the freedom to run wherever she wanted to go. Anytime the dog strayed too far, the owner called her name and she would come straight back. She had the discipline to be free. The second dog, however, had to be leashed and muzzled because he would wildly run about the park, jump on people, and take food from children and picnickers. He had none of the freedoms that discipline allowed.

Structure and discipline don't just make things easier on you. They make things easier on the whole team. It's much more comforting to work in an organized environment because everyone knows what's expected of them and what it takes to get the job done. Organization is basically a conduit for efficiency. In an unorganized environment, people are left to try to figure things out for themselves. When your team has to find their own way, they waste time and energy that could have been spent doing great work.

Enhance your navigational skills.

Problems are going to come up. That's inevitable. Your success and your team's success will depend on what you do about them. Leadership author Steve Ventura once said, "The hallmark of a well-managed organization is not the absence of problems, but whether or not problems are effectively resolved." That's why navigation is so important. It gives us the ability to correct our path instead of just pushing through the wrong one.

The best way to ensure you are properly navigating the implementation stage is to set timelines and checkpoints along the way. After you implement a process, it's not always easy to know when problems arise, so it's best if you build in a few points to check your progress. Problems are okay. They're just a part of anything we do. The key is to know they exist. Setting checkpoints allows you to uncover them sooner and work on navigating around them.

Navigation is a great skill for leaders to master for the improvement processes, but it's just as important for the people. It gives any team comfort to know that their leader is willing to find a way to overcome barriers in order to help everyone reach their goals. Leaders who aren't willing to alter their plans force their teammates to deal with problems that could otherwise be avoided. As a general rule, I try to be less flexible about the goal and more flexible about how to get there. I don't mind changing a plan if someone can show me a better way. Changing a plan is not a sign of weakness. It's a sign of good judgment.

Examine your processes.

Any business or organization who wants to stay ahead will find that sooner or later they will be asked to do more. The natural reaction during those times of change is to push people to work harder. The catch is that only works for so long. When you drive growth based on time and effort, you'll eventually run out of both. The clock only has 24 hours in any one day, and the human body can only expend a certain amount of energy before it shuts down. That's why we should continually review our processes to make sure they still make the best use of everyone's time.

A small change in a process can often result in more efficiency than a huge increase in effort. It's just that we don't always think in those terms. A lot of our processes become so routine that we often feel they can't be changed. Actually, I've found that making that type of change is pretty easy. All I have to do is ask two questions: "Who is doing it better than we are?" and "What are they doing?" There's always some person, some team, or some organization that has a better process. I want to know who they are and what they do. Then I want to know how we can do it.

Really, Next-Level Implementation Is...

...doing.

It doesn't seem like a "next-level" type realization, but a lot of people never stop talking and get started doing. You see, we all want to reach a great goal, but we can't finish what we never start. It's the people who commit to action who ultimately succeed in life. My dad always taught me that you can't control the stock market and you're not going to get all the breaks in life, but if you work hard enough for long enough, you can do just about anything you want. I'll have to say that his advice has served me pretty well.

A lot of leaders struggle with this concept, though. Not because they fear the work, but because they fear an imperfect plan. They want to keep planning until they're sure they have covered every possible scenario. In that type of environment, achievement is delayed because the work is delayed.

Billionaire entrepreneur Ross Perot once sold a company by the name of Electronic Data Systems to General Motors that was performing very well under his guidance, but quickly went downhill after the purchase. Perot was later asked why the company performed so well for him, but so poorly for GM. He said it was because of the difference between his organizational culture and theirs. He made a comparison to the old firearms protocol "Ready. Aim. Fire." He said that his strategy was "Ready. *Fire*. Aim." In other words, they would get to work and solve the problems as they went. He described the GM strategy as, "Ready. Aim. Aim. Aim. Aim. Aim…"

The perfect plan rarely exists. There comes a point when you just have to jump in and get started. When you are willing to get started, you give your teammates the chance to improve the plan and improve their skills. This approach allows the organization to be in a cycle of continuous improvement and achievement. The more your team does the more they'll learn, and the more they learn the more they'll achieve.

Authors David Bayles and Ted Orland tell a great story about the importance of learning by doing. It's about a ceramics teacher who divided his class into two equal groups. The first group would receive their grade based on the number of clay pots they produced. The other group would receive their grade based on the quality of only one pot. Based on those criteria, everyone assumed the best art would come from the quality group. In the end, however, the best pots came from the quantity group. The second set of students spent so much time focusing on the development of just one pot that they never spent time practicing. Since the first group made a lot of pots, they learned something each time they tried.

We can't be afraid to jump into action. People who do a lot will make a lot of mistakes, but they are also the people who are most likely to make a lot of successes. If you do less in order to limit your mistakes, you'll just do less. When it all comes down to it, all of the efforts to collect information, develop a plan, communicate, foster understanding, and set a direction are useless unless something gets done as a result. Some people talk about getting those things done and some people do them. Which one are you?

Next-Level Accountability

You cannot escape the responsibility of tomorrow by evading it today.

Abraham Lincoln

L eadership has been defined many different ways throughout history by researchers, scholars, and other leaders. Regardless of the definition, though, one aspect has remained the same: the leader is responsible for getting things done. Once any goal is set for a team or organization, there is an immediate expectation that everyone will do the work it takes to accomplish it. You cannot be in charge of a team without accepting accountability for the results of that work. Your team is only responsible for doing their job. You are responsible for the job. There's a big difference.

I learned my first lessons in accountability and responsibility on a dusty football field in Harlan, KY from my first and greatest mentor, J. B. Donahue. Coach Donahue taught us much more than just the game of football. He taught us to be young men, teammates, and leaders. By the time I was a senior, I was developing into one of the stronger leaders on the team. It was a role that I embraced and enjoyed, but it was one about which I had a lot to learn.

As the summer before my senior year progressed, I started noticing that Coach Donahue was scolding me more and more often. I knew I wasn't the best player on the team, but I really didn't think that

I was one of the worst. Further troubling me, he even began blaming me if someone else broke a rule or missed a blocking assignment. I couldn't understand why he was spending so much time singling me out, especially when I had no control over many of the things that upset him. One day I finally confronted him about it. I asked him what I needed to do to make things better.

What he said taught me a great deal. He told me that if I was going to lead that team, I would be accountable for their results; therefore, I had to be responsible for them. I had to take ownership of the players and their problems in order to make a difference. He told me I could only make a positive difference for the team if I felt as though my teammates' mistakes were my mistakes. He taught me that anytime I could make something my fault, I had the power to fix it. If I blamed something on other people I could do nothing but rely on them to solve the problem.

When you step into a leadership role, you don't have an option to shift accountability to other members of the team. Before that point, it was okay to just wait on someone else to choose a direction or make things right. However, once you are considered the leader you are out of that comfort zone. You now have the eyes on you while others are waiting to see what direction you will choose and what decisions you will make. The eyes are on you because you have the power to influence their lives, and as they say, with power comes responsibility.

I learned my second lesson in accountability as an assistant principal of a large, rural high school. This one had more to do with the effect of accountability on others. After dealing with disciplinary issues for the better part of a year, one thing became abundantly clear: the parents of the students that I saw repeatedly breaking the rules took no accountability for the actions of their children.

If I had to speak to a student more than once about a discipline problem, I would usually call the parents so they would know what their child was doing. Most parents were genuinely grateful to have had the opportunity to teach their child a better way. I seldom saw those kids or those parents in that office again. Some parents, however, felt that the problem was ours, not theirs. In fact, they usually blamed me, the teacher, the rules, the administration, society, Sponge-Bob SquarePants, and the governor. I saw those kids and those parents quite often.

The first set of parents felt the responsibility to make a positive difference in their children's lives and therefore seized the opportunity to correct the behavior. The second set of parents wanted to avoid that accountability; therefore, they also avoided the opportunities for improvement. When you accept the accountability for a problem, you want to work to solve it. When you don't, you try to explain it away or leave it for someone else.

It's much harder to succeed in life when you leave your problems for someone else, but it's impossible to lead by doing so. Accountability drives achievement. The things I have missed out on in my life have most often been because I didn't take enough responsibility to get them done. It would have been great if success would have just come to me, but that's not the way things work. That's not the way we should *expect* things to work. When we just expect things to come to us, we're going to be disappointed with most of our results.

Entrepreneur and author Mac Anderson believes that embracing an attitude of accountability is one of the most important life skills you can develop. He points to the following as some of the benefits of embracing accountability:

- You have more control over your destiny

- You become an active contributor rather than a passive observer

- Others look to you for leadership

- You gain a reputation as a problem solver

- You experience less anger, frustration, and helplessness

Think of how those traits could positively affect your life. Now think about how they could affect the lives of the people you lead. Remember, leadership is not about you. It's about your effect. If you want that effect to be positive, you have to accept your responsibility to help others grow, and you must embrace the accountability for their results.

Taking It to the Next Level: The True Responsibility of Leadership

Managers deal with processes. Leaders deal with people. That's why I believe it's a greater responsibility to lead than to manage. When you manage processes, you're responsible for the growth of numbers. When you lead people, you're responsible for the growth of lives and careers. Really, that's what makes the importance of accountability easy to understand. Leaders are expected to take care of the work, but more importantly they are expected to take care of the people. It's why the role of the leader exists in the first place.

We want accountable leaders because we want to know that the people in charge have as much invested in our success as we do. When leaders lack accountability, there is no guarantee that he or she will uphold the integrity of the work or the interests of the people. Peter Drucker once said, "I am amazed that today's prominent writers on leadership do not seem to realize that the three most charismatic leaders in all recorded history were named Hitler, Stalin, and Mao. I do not believe that there are three men who did more evil and more harm. Leadership has to be grounded in responsibility. It has to be grounded in a constitution. It has to be grounded in accountability."

The only way a leader can be a success is if her or his teammates are a success. Since you're in a position to affect the lives of other people, you have a responsibility to make that effect a positive one. Bestselling leadership author Ken Blanchard once wrote, "Good leaders are committed to helping their people win. When someone fails, they accept responsibility for that failure." Since your effectiveness is directly tied to their growth, you will have a lot at stake in their success. That's why Mr. Blanchard went on to say, "If your people are not performing well and you want to know why, step up to the mirror and take a peek."

Where We Go Wrong

We fear the accountability of failure.

Shooting to be average carries little risk, but who wants to strive for average? Performance is about accomplishment, and accomplishment comes with the risk of failure. How much you accomplish in life is directly related to the amount of risk you are willing to take. If you want to be a high achiever, you have to understand that the odds of failing are higher than they are for someone with lower expectations. When you don't fear the accountability of failure, you aren't afraid to make yourself accountable for more lofty goals and therefore give yourself a chance to accomplish them.

If you only try when you know the odds of success are great, you will fail less often, but you will also miss out on a lot of chances to succeed. For the most successful people in the world, failure is nothing more than part of the achievement process. Author William Saroyan believed, "Good people are good because they've come to wisdom through failure. We get very little wisdom from success, you know."

Personally, I reach very few of my goals. The minute it looks like I'm going to accomplish something, I raise my expectations. The honest fact is that I very seldom reach my final goal, so you could say that I fail at just about everything I do. In the end, though, I believe I will be more successful because I just keep shooting a little higher and trying a little harder. If I had been satisfied by reaching my initial goal, I might have failed less, but I wouldn't have accomplished nearly as much.

We think in terms of luck, fate, or chance.

There are a few ways to get what you want in life. One is hard work. The others are something along the lines of luck, charity, inheritance, and miracles. I prefer to stake my future on the work. It's the only element over which I have control. I can choose how hard I work; therefore, I can choose my odds for success. Thomas Jefferson agreed when he said, "I'm a great believer in luck and I find the harder I work, the more I have of it."

Luck, by its very nature, is a matter of chance. I don't like dealing with chance. That's another reason I really like accountability. It removes luck and chance from the list of factors that determine our success. Too many people like to think that others experience more success because they got lucky or had the right connections. That philosophy helps those people believe that they are not to blame for their lack of achievement. The truth is, though, a lot more people are successful because of the quality of their work than the quality of their luck. If you want to up your odds, you'll focus more on the former than the latter.

We get defensive.

Perhaps the biggest barrier to accepting accountability for our actions and results is the human tendency to become defensive. In fact, my definition of defensive behavior is an aggressive avoidance of accountability. When we act defensively, our only interest is explaining why something is not our fault. That type of behavior prevents us from doing what we should because we only focus on covering what was done. This often leads to an attempt to shift accountability away from ourselves. When people become defensive, they try to find ways to avoid, deny, or combat a shortcoming instead of dealing with it and moving forward.

The most common piece of defensive behavior I see from leaders today is an avoidance of responsibility for what their employees do. Avoiding that accountability is a major barrier to success because it's a barrier to the alignment of work and goals. When the leader shifts responsibility for a job to the employee, it means that leader is no longer committed to those duties. Without that commitment it's much easier to lose sight of both the work and the goals.

When I took charge of my first building as an administrator, my regional supervisor came for a surprise inspection. While walking through the facility, we came upon a garage door with a faulty hinge. He asked me who was responsible for that door. I was quite proud that even though I had only been there a few weeks I could already tell him which of the maintenance staff was responsible, so I quickly provided the man's name. My supervisor immediately replied, "Wrong! You are responsible! It's his job to fix it. It's your job to make sure it gets done."

How to Embrace Accountability

Don't make excuses.

Throughout my athletic career (what little of it there was), I saw a lot of quotes plastered on the walls of field houses, locker rooms, and weight rooms. One that always stuck with me was, "Excuses are a sign of weakness." I embraced that philosophy, and it really helped me train harder and push myself to be a better athlete, but it wasn't until many years later that I fully understood why it was so important to the rest of my life.

The fact is, excuses limit your potential. It's much easier to get from failure to success than it is to get from excuses to success. With failure there is no reason to quit. You just keep trying until you overcome the barrier. When you make excuses, you're basically letting yourself off the hook for whatever it was you were trying to do. That's no way to succeed. Avoiding your accountability for a mistake means you're not willing to fix it and the lost opportunity is never recovered. It takes a lot of strength to admit failure, but when you do, you can turn your attention to making up for the loss.

Above and beyond that, however, others have a hard time believing in you when you make excuses. Taking responsibility and accepting accountability makes it much easier for your teammates to believe that you can get them where they need to be. If you have the guts to own up to your faults and keep trying to work through them, it lets others know that you're willing to address any problems the team needs to overcome. I mean, how can they believe that you can solve their problems, if you're not willing to address your own?

Focus on the positives.

I think people often resist accountability because they only focus on its negative aspects. In all reality, the positives of accountability far outweigh the negatives. Accountability makes it much easier for us to accomplish the most important things in our lives. It interjects a healthy dose of pressure to keep us focused on what truly matters.

George Washington is often used as an example of character, vision, trust, respect, or influence, but one of his strongest attributes was his willingness to embrace accountability and use it to his advantage. Washington knew full well that people would be scrutinizing his every move. He made mention of it many times in his journals and letters. He even knew that his actions would be judged for hundreds of years due to the prominent positions he held. Because of this, he made certain that every decision he made and every action he took were the best they could be. He harnessed the power of accountability to make himself better.

I prefer to look at it this way. When things go wrong in a team environment, it's usually one of three things that caused the problem: 1) I chose the wrong direction; 2) I didn't prepare the people to do the job; or 3) They didn't perform. That means there's a 66.6% chance that any problem is mine. The good news is it also means there's a 66.6% chance that I have control over the solution.

Focus on the future.

Future problems don't go away by ignoring them in the present. If you want to solve a problem, you have to take ownership of it before you can fix it, and it's often easier to do that if you focus on the future you want rather than the situation you're in. We tend to avoid accountability because the moment when we first have to address our shortcomings is really uncomfortable, but if you can accept that moment as an opportunity to improve, you'll find it's easier to push through those tough times.

Once, while serving as a high school assistant principal, we had to suspend a basketball player just before the state tournament due to an incident involving him and several of his friends. I don't know exactly what happened, but the police had to remove him from a scene around midnight after we had won the regional title. It was not a good situation. What made it worse, though, was that a lot of people wanted us to ignore it and let him play.

He was a fine young man who just made a bad decision while riding the emotions of a big win. Since it didn't happen on school grounds or school time, I guess we could have let it go, but it wasn't the right thing to do nor was it the right message to send to our other students. All we could do was hope that everyone could move forward from that point. The problem was that while the young man never openly questioned the consequences, he never did anything to support them, either. The result was a shift in blame toward the administration for the decision rather than an acceptance of accountability for the action.★

Recently, I read a story of a similar account from a high school in Vermont. Five girls from a basketball team in St. Johnsbury were suspended for drinking alcohol at a New Year's Eve party. Even though school wasn't in session at the time of the party, when the coach found out what had happened she suspended the girls (four of them starters) because they had a strict "no alcohol" policy.

These girls, however, accepted accountability for their actions. At the very next basketball game they stood in front of the entire crowd and delivered the following message: "We hope you will understand that we are not bad kids. We made a mistake. What we did was definitely not worth it. We hope this event will make everyone open their eyes and realize that there is a big drug and alcohol problem in our community. If you work with us to try to solve this problem, you will help us feel that we have not been thrown off our basketball team for nothing."

In both cases, the immediate outcome was much the same. None of those young people were able to play basketball for the remainder of their seasons. Their effect, however, couldn't have been more different. By accepting accountability and moving forward, the young girls allowed everyone else to focus on improvement. By denying accountability, the young man allowed everyone else to focus on the negativity. Accountability helps you correct mistakes. Avoidance just keeps the problems hanging around.

★ I would like to add that the young man from this story learned a great deal from this experience and has grown up to be a fine role model for others.

When It All Comes Down To It, Next-Level Accountability Is...

...an internal locus of control.

For the most part, the good things in your life are the result of intentional efforts to make them happen. The quality of those efforts determines the quality of the outcomes. Accountability helps increase your odds of getting those positive results. People who hold themselves accountable for the outcomes of their decisions consistently outperform the ones who don't. That avoidance is what leads to faded dreams and unmet potential. It's the difference between taking control and just taking what life gives you. I want to take control because I'm not sure life has my best interests in mind.

The level of accountability you are willing to take for your own life is called your locus of control. The word *locus* is Latin for location. The phrase locus of control refers to whether you believe the things that control your life are located inside of you or outside of you. People who believe they control their circumstances are said to have an internal locus of control. Those who believe other people, situations, luck, or fate control their circumstances are said to have an external locus of control.

Former University of Connecticut psychology professor Julian Rotter first developed the concept of locus of control in the mid-1950s. Since that time, researchers and psychologists have been studying how people's locus of control affects their behavior and their resulting success. Individuals with a high internal locus of control have consistently been found to be more task-oriented and devote more of their time to the accomplishment of their goals. In fact, in many studies, it has been the most significant predictor of success.

By the 1990s, locus of control was being studied regarding its effect on leadership. The most common findings from these studies were that leaders who possessed an internal locus of control built more influence by building stronger relationships and greater respect. Basically, they found that having an internal locus of control makes it easier for people to follow you because they believe you have a greater chance of taking them to a better place.

Making the choice to embrace accountability and developing an internal locus of control is not easy, but it is a choice. If you want to give yourself the greatest chance to find fulfillment in your life, succeed in your career, and increase your ability to lead, you will want to cultivate a desire to be held accountable for your work and your goals.

If you start every project with a willingness to be responsible for the outcomes, you will find yourself much more committed to the work and much more likely to get great results in the end. Plus, if you never allow yourself to make excuses for any failed attempts, you will force yourself to grow even if those great results never materialize. Failure isn't meant to be explained away. It's meant to make you better. However, with an external locus of control you try to escape the responsibility and the failure, so you also escape the growth.

The key to overcoming any of the barriers we face in life is to take ownership of them and take control of what we do about them. Ultimately, the barrier isn't what stops us. It's our decision to stop trying that stops us. The most powerful thing about having a strong internal locus of control is that it puts you in charge of that decision. When you don't take that ownership, you allow about a million other variables to potentially stop you. When you do take that ownership, you are the only variable that matters.

Building Influence with Others

Working toward the right goals leads to success.

It only becomes leadership when others follow you.

Next-Level Attitude

*Things turn out best for the people who make the best
of the way things turn out.*

John Wooden

Our attitude plays a very important role in our approach to life,
our work, and the results. Many people really don't think attitude impacts success, but I absolutely believe that it does. Having a bad
attitude is like having a flat tire: you have to change it before you can
get anywhere. Your attitude is basically a self-fulfilling prophecy. In
other words, what you believe will happen is very likely to happen. If
your attitude is pulling you toward negative thoughts, you will be much
more likely to get negative results. If your attitude leads to positive
thoughts, you'll be much more likely to get positive results.

I believe people with good attitudes generally fall into one of
two categories: those who find a good attitude because things work
out for them, and those who find that things work out for them
because they have a good attitude. There's a big difference between
the two. The first group only has a good attitude when things are
going well, and since things don't always go well, they don't always
have a good attitude. The second group doesn't depend on outside
circumstances to maintain a positive outlook. They are determined to
keep the outside influences outside and manage the inside on their
own.

That approach is very often the key to building a platform for success. The quote to start this chapter came from the story of how Coach John Wooden came to be the head basketball coach at UCLA. During his tenure at that school he won over 600 games, ten national championships (including seven in a row), and six coach-of-the-year awards. He built a legacy at UCLA that will stand for decades and decades to come. Few people will ever think of UCLA basketball without thinking of John Wooden, and few people will ever think of John Wooden without thinking of UCLA basketball.

What most people wouldn't think is that Coach Wooden didn't want to be there. While he was very young in his career, he was teaching and coaching at Indiana State Teacher's College. After a successful season, he received two job offers in the same week. One was from UCLA, the other from the University of Minnesota.

Since Wooden was from the Midwest, he wanted the Minnesota job very badly. The only problem was that the university administrators wanted him to keep the outgoing coach on his staff as an assistant. Coach Wooden didn't consider that to be a good situation, so he told the athletic director he would accept their offer if they reconsidered that one condition. The director said they would let him know by 6:00 p.m. that Saturday. After the conversation, he called UCLA and told them that he would wait for Minnesota to make their decision, but he would let the UCLA administrators know whether or not he was coming by 7:00 p.m. that same Saturday.

The day of the decision a massive snowstorm hit the Great Lakes area and wiped out all communications in Minnesota. Coach Wooden, unaware of the situation, waited patiently for one hour past 6:00 for a call. Of course, the phone didn't ring until 7:00 p.m. when the UCLA athletic director called to see if Wooden had made up his mind.

Assuming Minnesota had decided to reject his terms, he told UCLA that he would be their next basketball coach. Shortly after that conversation, a Minnesota representative got through to Wooden to tell him of the power outage and that they had decided to accept his conditions. Coach Wooden was heartbroken, but told them he had accepted the position at UCLA and that no matter how badly he wanted to be at Minnesota, he would not go back on his word. He decided at that moment to make the best of the situation, even though it was far from the one he'd wanted. Ten national championships later, I'd say he did just that.

Many of the most successful people in the world have had to overcome similar barriers that could have led to destructive attitudes. Louis Armstrong, one of America's greatest jazz musicians, picked up his first trumpet in a juvenile detention center. Michael Jordan was cut from his basketball team in high school. Abraham Lincoln was demoted in the military and defeated in the majority of his first elections. Oprah Winfrey failed as a newscaster at age 22. Every one of them faced difficulties and bad situations, but each succeeded by making the best of the way things turned out.

We don't have to be high-profile public figures, though, to make those types of attitude choices. All of us have the ability to choose for ourselves. I've had to do it many times in my life and career. Things haven't always worked out for me like I thought they would. For example, I love my job in higher education. I love our mission, our connection to the workforce, and the impact we have on our students' lives, but this was never my plan. I wanted to be a football coach.

By the time I finished high school, I had no doubt that I was going to teach so I could be a coach. I enjoyed English, so I chose it as my major. When I graduated from college I took the first step toward my dream by getting a job as defensive coordinator for my hometown high school. I was on my way to a career as a high school football coach, and I was even going to get to do it at my alma mater.

The only problem was that my teaching job was not in English. There were no openings for an English teacher at our school, so my first job was teaching students with special needs as an emergency certified special education teacher. Since they had no other applicants for the vacancy, I was hired. I was nervous about teaching students with disabilities since I had no training in that area, but I looked forward to learning something new. To this day, those were the hardest working students I've ever known, and I loved being with them.

After that first year, the district had to reopen the position since I wasn't certified. When they received a qualified applicant the second year, I had to leave. My second job was teaching English at a school on the other end of the state. I didn't get to coach football because I had come to the district so late in the summer, but I was in a good place with good people. At the end of the first semester, I was informed that a position had opened up on the football staff, and they would like for me to take it. Life was good.

Things changed again, though, before I could ever step on the football field. I was asked to apply for an administrative position at the high school. I would be an assistant principal with a focus on discipline and facilities. It's really one of the worst jobs in a school district, but even though it was highly demanding and only dealt with other people's problems, I still enjoyed working with the teachers and the students.

Two years later I was asked to apply for a principal's position at an area technology center, which was a high school training facility for technical careers. I went to meet with the regional supervisor to tell him that I appreciated the offer, but I couldn't accept because I didn't know anything about technical education. Remember, I was an English-teaching football coach. These people were nurses, welders, electricians, and mechanics.

After seeing what they did at that school, though, I decided I would give it a shot. I got the job, and I found the most motivated teachers and students I had ever met. It was the first time in my life that education truly had an impact, a purpose, and a connection. I loved that job and still miss those people.

Again, two years later my career path changed. I was asked to consider an associate academic dean position at the regional community and technical college. Since I had experience in both liberal arts and technical education, it seemed like a good fit. I had to leave a very good job and would have to earn my Ph.D., but I was looking forward to the challenge. Ultimately, it led me to the most meaningful career I could have ever pursued. The work we do at the two-year college truly changes our students' lives. More importantly, it changes the lives of their children and their children's children.

Now, that's quite a bit of personal change over a small period of time. My job changed, my location changed, my focus changed, my impact changed, my path changed, and my goals changed. The one thing that didn't change? My attitude. I do consider myself lucky to have had those opportunities, but luck had nothing to do with what I made of them. The choices to be happy, to find the best in people, and to work hard were completely my own.

Australian pastor and author J. Sidlow Baxter wrote, "What is the difference between an obstacle and an opportunity? Our attitude toward it. Every opportunity has a difficulty and every difficulty has an opportunity." People don't succeed based on what happens to them. They succeed based on how they respond. When bad things happen, your attitude will largely determine that response. That's why things really do work out better for the people who make the best of the way things work out.

Taking It to the Next Level: Your Effect

While your attitude is important to you, its leadership application is much more significant. Your attitude doesn't just impact your success. It also plays a major role in determining just how easy you are to follow and the impact you can have on the people you lead. Leaders with a bad attitude are defensive, secretive, pessimistic, combative, unapproachable, directive, and usually resist change. Leaders with a positive attitude are more likely to be team-oriented, receptive, open-minded, approachable, and inclusive. Now think about how much easier it is to follow someone with those positive traits. More importantly, think about how much easier it would be for a team to succeed under that type of leadership.

Team success starts with the tone set by the leader. Her or his attitude is the first step in setting that tone. Everyone on the team takes more than just their direction from the leader. They take their approach to the direction. If you want everyone to take a positive approach to the work, you have to take a positive approach to them.

One of the best examples I've ever heard regarding the effect of a leader's attitude on team success came from two sea captains in the mid-1800s. During that time, the only means of international trade and travel were the open seas. Because of this, captains and explorers were constantly seeking better routes to navigate the Earth.

One of those routes took ships past the Auckland Islands just south of New Zealand. This route was advantageous because it was more direct, but very difficult due to the tight seams of water and the rocky sea floor. The harsh terrain caused many ships to crash and was considered one of the most dangerous routes in the world. Even if the crew escaped the sinking ship, the chances of surviving in that region were slim to none.

Once, in 1864, two ships got caught on the rocks and sank on opposite sides of the islands. The vessels were led by Captain Thomas Musgrave and Captain George Dalgarno. The captains and several sailors survived both crashes and made it to shore, but that's where the similarities ended. Captain Musgrave led his team with a strong will and a positive attitude. He made sure his men always believed they would make it home alive. They made the most of their time and strove every day to improve their situation. After 20 months on the island, they had secured enough resources to not only keep them alive, but to build a boat and sail to safety.

The crew led by Captain Dalgarno did not experience the same fate. He fell into a deep despair and his attitude spread throughout his team. He had given up all hope, and his team followed him. The prevailing attitude was "every man for himself," and after only three months all but three of the original 19 survivors had died.

Leadership must provide a path and a plan, but what truly makes either one work is the belief that our effort will lead to something positive. For that belief to be strong, the leader has to set the tone. Just like everyone else, your followers will choose whether or not to maintain a positive attitude and positive work ethic. Your attitude will either make it easier or more difficult for them to make a good choice.

Where We Go Wrong

We let stresses accumulate.

To maintain a good attitude and outlook, it's very important to reduce your level of stress. Stress has a negative impact on your attitude because it has a negative impact on your body. A report published by The Center for Disease Control indicated, "Anxiety, stress, and neurotic disorders are more severe than the average injury or illness. Affected workers experience a much greater work loss than those with all other injuries or illnesses." If you want to do your job well for many years, you have to find ways to minimize your stresses. If you want to help your teammates do their job well, you have to find ways to minimize theirs.

I love telling the story of Sergent York when I talk about stress. One of the legends of the World War I hero was that he took out an entire regiment of German soldiers by sneaking up behind them and picking them off one-by-one. Since he was shooting from the rear, he could take out the last soldier in the line without the man in front knowing what was going on. In this fashion, he just continued to eliminate soldiers until he had gotten them all.

It's a powerful metaphor for handling stress. You can't take on an entire month's worth of difficulties in one day, no more than one soldier could face an entire regiment head on. You can, however, deal with those stresses one at a time. With each stress you relieve, you'll find it's that much easier to keep a positive attitude about the rest of your life. If you make it easy for your teammates to eliminate their stresses, they will find it easier to keep a positive attitude about theirs.

We take an attitude of avoidance.

I came to know a vice president from a community college in Utah by the name of Troy Christensen several years ago while we were presenting at a conference in Richmond, Virginia. The title of his presentation was, "I Couldn't Fix the Brakes So I Made the Horn Louder." His point was that many leaders avoid really important problems by redirecting their attention to something a little less difficult or just ignoring the issue, altogether.

The issue with avoidance is that the solution to tough situations can usually be found in the problem. If you avoid that problem, you'll also avoid the solution. The best thing to do is put yourself right in the middle of the situation and ask, "How did I get here and what should I have done differently?" From that point you can ask, "How can I use that information to solve the problem?" By taking this approach, the mentality becomes a problem-solving attitude, not a problem-avoiding attitude. Avoiding your troubles doesn't make them go away. Avoiding troubles just keeps them hanging over your head.

We jump to conclusions.

Many times the things that put us in a bad mood or cause us emotional harm aren't even true. Conclusion jumpers spend more time than anyone in a foul mood because they don't even wait for all the facts before they form negative opinions and get upset. It's hard to feel good when you're constantly making negative assumptions about your future. It's even harder to lead with that kind of approach.

Jumping to conclusions is dangerous because you are creating realities for yourself. If you are misinformed, you're creating false realities; and leaders can't be effective by operating under false realities. To keep from getting upset by jumping to conclusions, I always advise folks to ask questions, and then choose a response. It's irresponsible to get upset about something before you know the whole story. You don't have a responsibility to like every direction or every decision, but you do have a responsibility to get all the information before you form an opinion.

How to Improve Your Attitude

Jump to conclusions.

I know. I just said that jumping to conclusions is often the wrong thing to do, but there's a way to make conclusion-jumping a positive thing. All you have to do is jump to positive conclusions! Many times we jump to negative conclusions because we are being overly critical or judgmental. When we are critical of others, it actually brings out the worst in ourselves because we assume the worst in them. If we can get to a place where we assume the best in other people, though, it will help us focus on the positives.

One of my favorite theories regarding the power of jumping to positive or negative conclusions in the leader/follower relationship was written by Douglas McGregor, which he called Theory X and Theory Y. Basically, McGregor proposed that Theory X leaders believe most people work because they have to, and if you are going to get anything out of them you have to push them all day long. Theory Y leaders, on the other hand, believe most people come to work wanting to do a good job; therefore, the leader just needs to provide the structure and support necessary for them to succeed.

Following this theory, it's easy to see how the leader's attitude matters to everyone else. If you jump to positive conclusions about the intentions of others, you will be much more likely to interact with them positively. If you jump to negative conclusions about their intentions, your relationship will likely be strained. Which attitude do you think would get the most from your teammates?

Change your focus.

You don't need the best of everything in order to *make* the best of everything. All you need is the right approach. When I got my first basketball goal, we didn't have a concrete driveway, so I had to dribble the ball on gravel. A few years later Dad built a carport in the back of the house, but it only extended to the middle of the goal. Of course, that meant I had a basketball court that was half concrete and half gravel. One of my friends came over to play one day, and when we went to play ball, he said, "I'm not playing on this. It's only half of a court." So he went back inside. I couldn't understand it. I was thrilled with my half-of-a-court!

How you view your circumstances will determine how you feel about them. Motivational speaker Tony Robbins teaches his clients that their focus drives their decisions because their focus drives their feelings. If you focus on a set of bad circumstances, you're going to feel sad, upset, or angry because your thoughts are continually bent toward those negative things. If you want to change the way you feel, all you have to do is focus on the good things in your life, instead. No matter how small or how few those positives may be, if they get the majority of your attention, you will naturally feel happier, more appreciative, and energized.

President Theodore Roosevelt once advised, "Do what you can, with what you have, where you are." If we can find ways to adopt this mindset, we will focus on making the best of our own situations. We won't waste time and energy longing for something we may never have. Wanting what you don't have can be a mental motivator if it inspires you to go out and work for it. On the other hand, wanting what you don't have can be a mental poison if it makes you resent everything else.

Find the best in people.

It's not always easy to get the best out of everyone because it's not always easy to *find* the best in everyone. You have to remember that your job is not limited to only helping the people you like. Your job is to help everyone. My personal philosophy in this regard is to find a way to "love above" the annoyances and difficult attitudes in others. It's not easy, but I know that down deep I love the people much more than I dislike the way they sometimes act. All I have to do is stay focused on that mindset so I can keep a positive outlook about my relationship with them.

Nelson Mandela took a very similar approach, and wrote in his autobiography that he was often tempted to lash out at his tormentors during his years of imprisonment through the apartheid in South Africa. He said he fought that urge by looking for that one glimmer of goodness in them to restore his faith that ultimately there is some good in everyone, and all they needed was for someone to help them grow it. Keeping this perspective was the only thing that kept him going in a positive direction through those difficult years. Ultimately, it allowed him to return to his country as a much better leader.

Finding the best in others makes life so much easier. When you focus on the positive attributes of those around you it's easier to focus on your own positives. Most of the people I've met who have a bad attitude seem to focus on the worst in others and the reasons those people are bringing them down. They think their bad attitude is a result of everybody else's. Here's a good rule of thumb regarding that philosophy: if you have a problem with everybody else, everybody else is not the problem.

Take time to rejuvenate.

Any of us can only maintain a positive attitude under tough circumstances for so long. Eventually, we reach a point where we feel burnt out and start to lose our motivation and our purpose. It's also the point where we lose our productivity and patience with others. That's why we need to occasionally step away from work or a project for a little while and come back to it when we can make more efficient and effective use of our time.

My best advice is this: take time to play. Sometimes it's hard to relax and get your mind off things, but when you play, you only focus on having fun. Dr. Stuart Brown, a psychiatrist who studied the positive attributes of play, asserts that the human body and spirit is not intended to continually operate without some sort of release. He says, "The opposite of play is not work. It is depression, so play might well be considered a survival skill."

When It All Comes Down to It, Next-Level Attitude Is...

...self-control.

Strong attitudes are consistent attitudes, and consistency is one of the traits we look for in our leaders because consistency is a strong indication of self-control. When you maintain a strong sense of self-control over your responses and behaviors, it means you are <u>in</u> control. I don't know about you, but when I choose to follow someone I want to believe they are in control of what they're doing.

Having that type of control helps everyone believe that you will be more likely to help them get through any problems and much more likely to help them achieve their goals. No one wants to follow emotional instability, negativity, or pessimism. Why would they? Remember, one of the principles of Next-Level Leadership is that we want to make it easier on others to follow us. Choosing a solid, positive attitude does just that.

The good news is that you are in charge of your attitude. It really is a choice. In fact, it may be the only choice over which we have complete control during the course of our day. The sooner you come to think of it that way, the sooner you can choose a good one. I didn't always embrace that philosophy, but I learned its true power from my Uncle Walt. He taught me that we don't have to let outside fights impact our inside lights.

Uncle Walt was one of my biggest heroes. He was a deputy sheriff with a fleet of coal trucks and a joke for every occasion. To a young mountain boy, he was one of the coolest people in the world. He had big trucks, big guns, and a heart the size of Texas. He always had time for me, and he always made me feel like a million dollars.

When I was around 22 years old, though, Walt was diagnosed with cancer. It became very aggressive, and his last days were pretty tough on him. On one of the last visits I had with him I could tell he was in great pain, and I didn't know if I could stand to be there much longer. Walt must have sensed my discomfort. He calmed himself, looked at me with his little devilish grin, and asked, "Did I ever tell you about the time your dad got stuck in a tanker car and we had to cut him out with a blowtorch?"

Walt fought cancer very hard, but it was a fight he couldn't win. The last time I spoke to him on the phone, his voice was faint, but somehow strong. I asked him how he was feeling, and he said, "My light's still shining." Now, if Uncle Walt's light was still shining in spite of all he was fighting, how in the world can I let snippy comments and daily drama flicker my flames? Our outside fights don't have to put out our inside lights, but it's a choice each of us has to make for ourselves. I hope yours is a good one.

Guiding Lights to get Your Attitude Right

Help someone else to help yourself.

Avoid gossip and drama like the plague.

Surround yourself with positive people.

Never blame others for the bad things that happen to you.

Express gratitude whenever you feel it.

Make a commitment each morning to have a good day.

Next-Level Trust

The glue that holds all relationships together – including the relationship between the leader and the led – is trust.

Brian Tracy

Trust is often considered one of the most important aspects of leadership because it's a pathway to elements like integrity, relationships, respect, and influence. We have to realize, though, that trust is not just a pathway to other elements. It's a result of many others. Specifically, it's a result of time spent doing the right things, the right way, for the right reasons. Trust isn't just a tool for leaders to pull out when they need it. It has to be earned before it can be used. The trick is we don't build trust by developing our trust skills. We build trust by developing the skills that allow us to be trusted.

Developing those skills is crucial to building a high-achieving team. When you build a strong bridge of trust between you and your team, the bond between the leader and the follower doesn't have to be questioned and the team can focus on doing what they need to do. When this happens a team's potential is high. When the bond of trust is weak, however, that potential is much lower because your team-mates will be hesitant to follow the directions you choose.

Trust is more important today than it has ever been. The old model of business and leadership was founded on processes, competition, power, and profit. Those structures were based on a clear hierarchy and a strict observance of authority. The goal was set, the process was explained, and the chain-of-command was sacred. Employees didn't have to trust their superiors; they just had to know what those superiors expected of them so they could get to work.

Today, the business model has changed. The modern organizational world depends on a strong foundation of trust. Organizations are built on integrity, relevance, relationships, influence, understanding, and tolerance of change. Vertical structures of authority are becoming less and less effective. People have to believe in their work and believe in each other before they will be motivated to work together toward a common goal.

Many leaders still take trust for granted though. They assume followers should trust them based on the position they hold. At one point in history that may have been true, but after years of scandals, fraud, unethical behavior, let-downs, and poor performance, the world's innate trust of leadership has all but faded away. What was once taken as an understanding of the leader/follower relationship must now be earned over the course of time.

Take the American government's involvement in the Vietnam War, for instance. The conflict ended badly in Vietnam and caused a great deal of civil unrest in America. What many people forget, however, is that a full two-thirds of the American people supported U. S. involvement before the war. They felt it was the right thing to do and the right place to fight communism on a global stage. President Lyndon B. Johnson and his staff had a great deal of support. So what changed?

Over the course of the years following the start of the conflict, the Johnson administration delivered half-truths to the American public and continued to follow a poorly constructed plan, even after they realized it was the wrong thing to do. They were caught in a web of deceit and tried to fight their way out of it by presenting a false reality. Over time they were fooling fewer and fewer people, and more and more of them were losing faith in their government.

In the end, too much trust had been lost. To be honest, we're still fighting that battle today in American politics. After scandals in the administrations of Presidents like Nixon and Reagan and poor choices made by Presidents like Clinton and Bush, the American public's level of trust for leadership is mighty low.

The most important thing to realize is that everything just works better when the team trusts their leader. Popular motivational speaker Cavett Roberts says, "If my people understand me, I'll get their attention. But if my people trust me, I'll get their action." Leaders must inspire action; therefore, leaders must build trust. Whether that position is CEO, team leader, husband, mother, or advisor, your ability to function in any supervisory capacity depends on the level of trust others have placed in you.

When it all comes down to it, we earn trust in two ways: doing the things we're supposed to do and doing them the right way. When you do what you're supposed to do, people can trust your work. When you do those things the right way, people can trust you.

Taking It to the Next Level: Empowerment

Trust is one of the most powerful elements of leadership, but you should always remember that trust is a two-way street. All too often we only focus on the skills that allow others to trust us, but it's what we do to show our teammates we trust them that often defines the relationship. To maximize our team's potential and fully develop them as individuals, we have to provide opportunities for them to succeed on their own. It's the best way for them to learn and grow and the only way they can earn the trust that will lead to their own respect and influence. We have to give them chances to lead their own projects; then we need get out of their way and let them prove they can do it. In other words, we must empower them.

Mid-19th century educator and civil rights activist Booker T. Washington once said, "Few things help an individual more than to place responsibility upon him, and to let him know that you trust him." Empowerment is tough for a lot of leaders because they are essentially giving away control over something by which they will ultimately be judged. If you prepare people to do their job, however, and give them the flexibility to work to their strengths they will be very likely to represent you well. In fact, I've found that my teammates usually do it better than I could have, anyway.

It's a concept that applies to any team, no matter how small or large. In the early 1980s, the designers at Ford Motor Company were extremely dissatisfied with the new Thunderbird, but it was the only model that met the company's rigid product-design standards. The leaders at Ford delegated a good deal of the work, but empowered no one to do it as they saw fit. When Donald Petersen came on board as the new Chief Operating Officer, he changed all of that. He told the design team to build a car they would be proud to drive, and to build it using their own parameters. Not only did that team build a groundbreaking Thunderbird, they used some of the innovations to unveil the best-selling car in America that year, the Ford Taurus.

For empowerment to make a difference, it has to move beyond delegation. When you delegate, you give someone a job. When you empower, you give someone control. Assigning work is just the beginning. It's not just a job we try to improve through empowerment. It's the people. The employee is responsible for the success of the project, but the leader is responsible for the success of the employee.

The important thing to remember is that for empowerment to succeed, we have to make sure we provide an environment where employees receive the support they need to set them up for success. We have to provide the authority to take control of the project, the accountability for its results, and the resources to be successful. For a better look at why each of these elements is important, take a look at the following empowerment formulas:

Opportunity + Authority + Accountability + Resources = Empowerment

Opportunity + _____ + Accountability + Resources = Micromanagement

Opportunity + Authority + _____ + Resources = No Commitment

Opportunity + Authority + Accountability + _____ = Frustration

Only the top formula leads to successful empowerment, but too many leaders fail to address every component. It takes more than just the opportunity to lead a project to help others learn to lead and learn to succeed. When you withhold the authority to take control of the work, you will micromanage their efforts to lead on their own. If you don't establish clear accountability, you will often stifle the commitment it takes to drive completion. And if you fail to provide the resources necessary to do the job, you'll be setting them up for failure from the very start.

If you get it right, though, you will build your employees' skills and also build stronger connections with them. Nothing builds a bond between the leader and the follower like the trust that's given through empowerment. Everyone knows that the leader will still be accountable at the end of the day, so they know it's more than just a project with which they have been trusted. It's your reputation that's on the line. When you delegate a job to someone, you let them know you trust them with the work. When you empower someone to do that job, you let them know you trust them.

Where We Go Wrong

We expect trust to come with the title we hold.

Too many supervisors just expect their followers to trust them when they make decisions, set goals, and lead change merely because of their position. Trust just doesn't work that way. People trust a person, not a position, and our position doesn't define who we are. As my sociologist friend Russ Ward once told me, "We don't own our status. We just rent it for a little while. What we truly own is who we are beneath the titles."

In their book, *Leader as Coach*, David Peterson and Mary Dee Hicks outline the five main responsibilities of a leader. The first is to Forge a Partnership. Forging a partnership means that you must build a leader/follower relationship, and those are not easy to build. It takes a great deal of time and effort to forge a partnership because those types of connections only come when you know people well enough to understand them, and they know you well enough to believe in you. If you don't take that time it will be very difficult to build a following. Followers can't trust a leader they don't know, and they won't follow a leader they can't trust.

We think honesty means not lying.

Nothing will breach trust quite as fast as a lie. I think just about everyone in the world understands that. Likewise, just about everyone in the world knows that telling the truth is the right thing to do. The problem is that not everyone knows just exactly where the line is drawn between the two.

Because that line can sometimes get blurry, many good people struggle with honesty. They don't necessarily struggle with the black and white issues, but the gray areas cause some trouble. You have to be aware of the types of dishonesty that can occur between you and your team if you want to uphold the integrity of the position. Here are a few of the most common types of dishonesty as they apply to leadership:

Withholding information to protect someone's feelings: The number one violation of honesty is keeping the hard truths about performance or behavior from teammates. You will never add value to your team if your desire to avoid hurt feelings is stronger than your desire to help them improve. Keeping information from someone that would allow them to improve their skills or their reputation is just as harmful as any lie a leader could tell.

Saying nothing: Many folks just don't see anything wrong with not sharing information. I mean, how can you tell a lie if you don't tell anything? Withholding information, however, can be just as damaging if sharing it would be beneficial.

Perpetuating unconfirmed stories (otherwise known as gossip): Gossip may just be the eighth deadly sin. Although most gossip-spreaders don't knowingly tell lies, leaders are held to a higher standard. If you don't know something is true, you'd be irresponsible to spread it. People should be able to take the leader's word as fact.

Half-Truths: Remember, a half-truth is also a half-lie. When it comes to little white lies and half-truths, there's honest, then there's everything else.

We make too many promises.

The act of making promises is a very important commitment in any relationship. You have to realize that every promise is a chance to build trust by following through on what you say. Unfortunately, every promise is also a chance to lose trust by not doing what you said you would do. Many leaders become hallway heroes by walking around and promising everything under the moon. When they get back to the office, however, they forget about all those promises or find that they're unable to follow through.

You have to be careful about what you say because what you say becomes what you're committed to do. It's impossible to build credibility and trust if you don't follow through on those commitments. It feels good in the moment to promise someone what they want or what they need, but from that moment forward it becomes the new expectation – and you can't be trusted if you continually fall short of your expectations. If you want to be successful, follow through on your promises to yourself. If you want to be trusted, follow through on your promises to everyone else.

How to Do Better

Build a bridge of trust between you and your team.

When you have a bridge of trust between you and your team, you have a firm connection with them, even when times are tough. It keeps you from being isolated from each other when you most need unity. The illustration below represents the elements on which you need to concentrate to build a strong bond with your teammates. When these elements are strong, it's easy to build your bridge, and you can overcome the troubled waters many teams must cross.

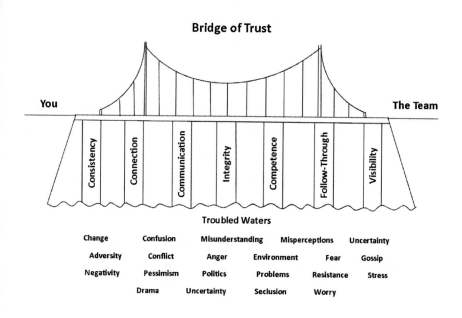

Bridge of Trust

You   The Team

Consistency   Connection   Communication   Integrity   Competence   Follow-Through   Visibility

Troubled Waters

Change	Confusion	Misunderstanding	Misperceptions		Uncertainty
Adversity	Conflict	Anger	Environment	Fear	Gossip
Negativity	Pessimism	Politics	Problems	Resistance	Stress
	Drama	Uncertainty	Seclusion	Worry	

You can see that the center pylon under the bridge is integrity. Without integrity, trust is impossible. You can't earn someone's trust unless they believe the core of your character is built on strong moral and ethical values. People may trust your intelligence or ability if they doubt your integrity, but they will never trust you. I believe that an honest life is an easy life, but more importantly, I believe an honest life is an easy life for everyone else to follow.

The other elements supporting the bridge are very important, as well. When it comes to completely earning the trust of your teammates, you can't remove any pillar and expect to maintain a solid foundation. Let's take just a minute to look at how each pillar supports the bridge you must build with your team:

Consistency: People can't trust you if they never know what to expect from you. When you are not consistent, you are not dependable. No one trusts a leader they can't count on to come through for them.

Connection: The bond of trust is just that: a bond. When you connect with your teammates you let them know that you care for them, and caring is the most powerful form of trust.

Communication: Without communication, people have no way of knowing they can trust you. When you communicate, you prove your commitment, demonstrate competence, clarify direction, and give people a reason to believe in you. When you don't communicate, people are left to figure those things out for themselves.

Competence: No one will trust your ability to make decisions about their work until they trust you know something about it.

For example, my wife, my doctor, and my leaders all impact my life. Each of them will make decisions about my future and I want to trust that those decisions will be for the best. Your team will want the same from you.

Follow-Through: Follow-through is your credibility with your team. That credibility is largely based on whether or not you do what you say you're going to do. If your team can't believe in your word, they won't believe in you.

Visibility: This one's pretty simple. It's hard to trust what you don't see.

Be as transparent as possible.

Transparency is another element that makes trust and trustworthiness much easier. When everyone knows what you're doing it's much easier for them to believe you're doing the right things, and that you're doing them the right way. Transparency means that no one has to make assumptions about how you spend your time, and the fewer assumptions your teammates have to make, the smaller the chance they'll jump to the wrong conclusions.

Transparency strengthens your relationships by making it much easier for your teammates to trust you, but it also strengthens the work by allowing everyone to support each other. When everyone knows what is really going on, they can fully contribute relevant ideas and use their strengths to help cover weaknesses. If you only give your teammates part of the story, you'll find that you limit their potential to help.

Let people tell you what they think.

One of the best trust lessons I've ever learned was taught to me as a young assistant football coach under J. B. Donahue. J.B. taught us that we could argue, fuss, and fight behind closed doors, but once we left the coach's office, we had to be on the same page. He always encouraged us to disagree with him so we could come to the *best* conclusions, not just *his* conclusions. Very often he changed his point-of-view because of what we shared. Because of this, we trusted that when Coach Donahue made a decision, he had truly considered all the options and made the best decision for all of us, even if it wasn't always the one we wanted.

It's a principle shared by General Colin Powell. The General always told his subordinates, "Disagree with me, do it with feeling, try to convince me you are right. You owe that to me. That's why you're here. But don't be intimidated when I argue back. A moment will come when I have heard enough and I make a decision. At that very instant, I expect all of you to execute my decision as if it were your idea."

People will trust you and support your direction more readily if they know you will let them help you make your decisions. That support will make the choice work, not the choice itself. Leaders must listen, but at some point, they must unify. Just remember that it's easier for people to unify in the end if you've included them from the beginning.

Basically, Next-Level Trust Is...

...credibility.

Have you ever thought about the importance our society places on credibility? We all want to know who someone is before we care what they say. It's why people place a good deal of importance on introductions. Authors and speakers are often introduced as "Leader in the Field," "Best-Selling," or "Expert." Actors are often introduced as "Academy Award Winning" or even "Academy Award Nominated." Athletes are introduced as "World Champ" or "Hall of Famer." Those introductions are made because people try to build credibility so they will be taken seriously.

It's the same with leadership. Without credibility, no one will pay a lot of attention to you or what you tell them. The only difference is that nobody introduces us. We introduce ourselves by the things we say and do each day. If you want your teammates to care about what you have to say and the direction you want to take, you have to continuously prove that you're worth following.

Every phase of leadership improves when those who follow believe they can trust the leader. For their book, *The Credibility Factor*, James Kouzes and Barry Posner researched the effect of credibility on a leader's influence and effectiveness. They found that employees worked harder, were more engaged in their job, and took ownership in the organization when they felt as though they worked for a credible leader. Given those findings, it's easy to see how credibility matters if we want to add value to the lives of others.

Just remember that like trust, credibility must be earned. It doesn't come with a position. When your actions and decisions consistently demonstrate a commitment to integrity and success, people will feel good about you and will take comfort in knowing they can expect you to come through for them. Still, you can't expect to be perfect. Eventually you will make some mistakes. If you want to maintain credibility, you must be willing to admit those mistakes and move forward. I adopted this mindset because I'd rather be wrong than lose credibility.

Think about that last statement for a second. I said I'd rather be wrong than lose credibility. Many leaders think that being wrong is how you lose people's trust, but that's not necessarily true (unless you're wrong a lot more than you're right…). Everyone will make mistakes, and everyone will eventually make a bad decision. It's what you do about them that will help or hurt your credibility. Making a bad decision is not the worst thing that can happen to you. *Staying* with a bad decision is the worst thing that can happen to you. That's what leads to distrust. It's easier to keep credibility by making a mistake than to keep credibility by trying to make a mistake work.

In the end, your credibility will determine how far others will follow you into the realm of the new and different. If you want to make it easier on the people who have chosen to follow you, give them every reason to believe in you so they won't have to doubt your direction. When you have credibility, your teammates know you have the ability to come through for them, but more importantly, they believe that you will.

Next-Level Relationships

No one cares how much you know until they know how much you care.

John C. Maxwell

The strength of your relationships with your teammates will affect all three phases of leadership. Whether we're talking about choosing direction, aligning work with goals, or building influence, your ability to work with people will determine how well you do your job. Teams choose better directions when they do it together; they connect with the work more easily when they connect with each other, and influence only comes through the trust and respect a leader earns with the followers.

At one time, people only needed to identify with their work to feel productive and fulfilled. This made the organization the most powerful force. You didn't necessarily have to build relationships to motivate those groups of workers. The work or the need for work drove them to perform whatever task was assigned by the supervisor. Today, it's a different story. People will work just as hard as they ever have, but they will do it for different reasons. Today, people have to know why they do the work and why they should follow the leader.

Now, you may or may not agree with this new culture, but you don't have to agree with culture to adapt to its norms. The fact of the matter is that no leader or company can succeed without great people. If you can't connect with those people, you are the one who becomes irrelevant, not them. As bestselling business author Daniel Pink puts it, "Talented people need organizations less than organizations need talented people." That's why we have to focus on developing strong relationships with our teams. Jobs won't keep great employees anymore. Relationships will.

Taking It to the Next Level: The Leader/Follower Relationship

The most successful leader/follower relationships are most like those built between coaches and their players. Those connections differ from friend/friend relationships because they are less about social interaction and more about nurturing growth. There is an undeniable bond between players and coaches, yet those relationships are seldom seen as friendships. They contain the same elements of caring and respect, but add extra dimensions of depth with structure and mentorship. When the leader allows friend/friend relationships, it's not as easy for the follower to accept the guidance and supervision necessary for growth and achievement.

Coaches, like any leader, have many different styles with which they organize their teams and interact with their players. The successful ones all share certain traits, however. Basically they all unify purpose, provide structure, improve ability, and motivate performance. (Sounds a lot like what any leader should be doing, huh?)

Unify Purpose

The first job of a coach or leader is to unify purpose. Humorist Will Rogers once wrote, "Everyone is ignorant, only on different subjects." It's true when you think about it, and it's a great reason to become a member of a team. Everyone has weaknesses. Coaches who unify their team's purpose allow each member to play to his or her own strengths while using everyone else to cover for the weaknesses. That's why teams are stronger than a collection of individuals. An individual cannot be as strong when they have no one to help them overcome their weak areas.

Provide Structure

The leader is charged with providing the discipline it takes to create structure. Some people have the ability to excel in a loosely organized environment, but many people need well-defined parameters to usher them toward success. That's what structure and discipline are intended to do. When you provide an atmosphere of discipline, you make it easier to do the work today that will lead to success tomorrow. Without that structure, people may not choose to use their time and energy doing the things that will lead to something better.

Improve Ability

We tend to think that successful coaches are the ones who win a lot of games. While that may be the easiest measure of coaching success, it's not necessarily the best one. I think the true measure of success for any coach is simply this: did the players reach their potential?

For the great coaches, it's not always about the player who rushes for 1,000 yards or hits 20 home runs in a season. It's about whether or not that player did better than they could have because of the effort they gave in the preparation.

Leaders should judge themselves by the same criteria. Your team is probably not going to reach every goal you set, and they may not always be the best in their field, but if you add value to them and they consistently improve over time, you should consider your time together a great success. The thing is people don't always have the internal drive to improve on their own. If you don't make efforts to raise their ability they may never be any better than they currently are. Regardless of the final product, that would be a loss in my book.

Motivate Performance

You can give an order to do something, but you can't necessarily give an order that someone gives it their all. That requires motivation. Some leaders don't see the value in motivation because they think it's only a short-term fix, but as leadership consultant Zig Ziglar says, "People often say that motivation doesn't last. Well, neither does bathing. That's why we recommend it daily." Motivation is like the grease on the wheels of achievement. Ability may set our teammates' potential, but desire helps them reach it.

The best coaches use a variety of techniques to increase that desire. These can include pushing someone a bit harder, patting them on the back, rousing speeches, or appeals to the heart. In my opinion, though, the greatest motivator of all is sincere appreciation and praise for a job well done. Even though discipline and constructive feedback are large parts of a coach's repertoire to enhance skills, we can never forget about the power of positive praise. If you don't spend enough time patting someone on the back when they've done well, it's hard for them to believe you care when you're smacking their hand when they've done wrong.

Where We Go Wrong

We don't put in the work.

Relationships are not always easy. In fact, they're rarely easy. It takes a lot of work to stay closely connected to someone for a long period of time. It's why the divorce rate is so high. When couples are in the dating phase, the entire relationship is built on fun and excitement. When they become husband and wife, however, they have to share responsibility and build a future. Those roles take a lot more effort. When people tell me that their marriage isn't working, I ask them, "Is the marriage not working or are you not working?"

Marriages and teams don't fail during the good times. They fail when times get tough. It's easy to survive the honeymoon stage of any relationship, whether we're talking about newlyweds or a newly hired leader. We tend to see the best in each other and everyone is putting their best foot forward. Shortly after the honeymoon, though, we find some annoyances or misaligned priorities, personalities, or philosophies. That misalignment often leads to disagreement.

At this point, people have to try a lot harder to get along than they initially did. Oftentimes, though, they just wait for the problems to go away. When things don't improve (and they won't) they get tired of waiting. That's when the aggravation turns into resentment and the relationship is in trouble. This pattern can be broken at any point, however, with the addition of three elements: confrontation, communication, and compromise. Problems in relationships are like any other problems – they have to be addressed before they go away. If you're willing to communicate and compromise, you stand a chance to make things better. If you're willing to do neither, you might just stand alone.

Leaders have to put in the work to build strong relationships. They don't just happen. Before people will want you to succeed, they must know that you want them to succeed. If you want respect, you must give respect. If you want honesty, you must be honest. If you expect them to be open to your ideas, you must be open to theirs. All in all, if you find that you're struggling in your leader/follower relationships, the problem is likely not what you're getting out of them, but what you're putting into them.

We use power techniques instead of people techniques.

Power techniques are about pushing people toward goals, and leaders shouldn't push people around. They're supposed to lead, and they're supposed to do it by developing relationships. You've probably heard the old saying that you catch more flies with honey than vinegar, but I think it's equally important to consider an old Southern proverb: never cut what you can untie. It's not always about bringing people to you with the honey. It's about not damaging a connection that you may come to depend on later.

It's a lesson Pat Summitt learned early in her career. Most of us know Coach Summitt as the highly successful, highly intense former basketball coach of the Tennessee Lady Vols. She rose to prominence during an era when women's and men's athletics received equal priority among college athletic offices and national media coverage. When she was building her program in the 1970s, however, she was far from a superstar. She was an unknown coach in the underappreciated world of women's basketball.

The discrimination she faced as a part of women's sports in those years was maddening, yet she knew that if she approached the injustices she faced (such as low budgets, poor facilities, and no practice gear) with aggressive behavior, she would lose the support she hoped to receive in the future. Instead, she was thankful for what she got, made sure that her superiors knew she was working hard, and never made people feel that she was their enemy. By doing so, she never damaged the relationships that later allowed her to build a championship program.

Confrontation is handled poorly.

Leaders who want to improve their teammates' skills and abilities know that great performance should be recognized, but they also know that poor performance must be confronted. Without that intervention those employees continue to harm themselves and the team. If you want to help someone improve, you have to let them know what they're doing wrong and what they must change in order to get better.

When this type of conflict between right and wrong exists, it's your duty to resolve it. Another name for conflict-resolution is problem-solving. Leaders who avoid resolving conflict are leaders who avoid solving problems. Many people view confrontation as a bad thing, but it's actually a very positive thing when handled properly. Conflict, by its very nature, means there is a misalignment between people or processes. It only becomes a negative force when the majority of the resolution efforts are focused on the problems. To become a more positive force, the objective should always be correction and improvement.

Always remember that the purpose of confrontation is to build people up, not tear them down. If you want to handle conflict in a positive manner, follow these simple guidelines:

Never make it personal: One of the most important aspects of confrontation is that we take issue with the problem, not the other person.

Pick your battles: Not every fight is worth the fight.

Confront problems early: If you don't, they may become habits; and habits are more personal and harder to break.

Focus on improvement: The intent is not just to stop negative behavior, but to start positive behavior. Focusing on the problem does nothing to initiate a solution.

Be specific: You have to know enough to discuss specific improvements. People improve at a fundamental level, and fundamentals are details.

End with a plan: You can't just talk about what should be done differently. To be successful, you have to define the steps.

If I have one secret to confrontational success, though, it's that I always try to provide a way out. I try to let the employee have the last word when possible so they have some control over the outcome. I may tell them what needs to be done and let them tell me how they're going to make it happen, or I might provide two or three options and let them pick which one they want. When people feel as though they have some control over the path, they will be much less likely to resist the new direction.

How to Improve Your Relationship Skills

Take the Leadership Point-of-View.

To develop strong connections, you have to take the Leadership Point-of-View and look at the world through the eyes of other people. I've found that when I struggle with relationships it's usually because I've looked at the world through my eyes. The most important aspect of the leader/follower relationship is not based on what the leader believes to be important. It's based on what the followers believe to be important. We have to realize that everyone lives within their own world, and each of those worlds has different priorities, fears, values, goals, and realities. When relating to another person, you have to keep in mind that the things you consider to be trivial or inconsequential may matter a great deal to them.

I remember once while serving as an assistant principal, I was preparing for a meeting to terminate a maintenance employee when I got a call from the local police department. They were on their way to arrest a student who had stolen an ATV the night before. Either of those events would have been enough to create some stress, but the combination of the two brought things to a whole new level. While I was stepping out the door to go inform my principal, a young teacher stopped me because she had a major problem.

She grabbed me by the arm and told me that once again Little Johnny had come to class without a pencil. I laughed and handed her a pencil. I certainly had more pressing issues than a forgotten pen. I later found out, however, that she broke down and cried after I left. I didn't take into account the seriousness of her problem as it related to her world. As it compared to taking someone's livelihood or arresting a student, it seemed petty to me, but as it related to her ability to run her classroom, it was very important to her. Even though I had to address the other issues first, I could have at least assured her that she was important to me and that I would come to see her as soon as possible.

It was her world I should have been concerned with. Not mine. My mistake was not made in the managerial process of setting priorities. It was made in the way I handled the relationship with the young teacher. I had an opportunity to help her overcome a problem and build a stronger connection with her, but I chose to focus on my problems without even acknowledging hers.

As it applies to relationships, the Leadership Point-of-View is all about empathy. Empathy is basically the ability to respond to someone's needs based on a compassionate understanding of their situation. When you care enough to understand someone and respond to their needs based on that understanding, you let them know that you truly care for them.

Success in leadership begins and ends with success in relationships. There's no doubt that processes are important, but processes will never work for you. People will work for you. You will find that it's much easier to have a people focus and win with procedures than it is to have a procedure focus and win with people.

Make people feel good about themselves.

If you want people to feel good about following your directions, they first have to feel good about following you. You can help people feel good about following you by working to improve your charisma skills. I didn't always believe that charisma was an important leadership trait, but a dear mentor of mine by the name of Jeff Hockaday once told me, "Juston, leadership is easier when the people you lead like being with you. They will want you to succeed, and your success is their success. Of course, their success is your success. You see, when they like you the whole thing works better."

Charisma has received a bit of a bad reputation over the years because folks tend to confuse charm and charisma. Many people even use the two terms interchangeably, but there is a big difference. Charm is what you use to make people feel better about you. Charisma is what you use to make people feel better about themselves.

Charisma can manifest itself in many different ways. Some charismatic leaders, like John F. Kennedy, inspire hope. Some, like Oprah Winfrey, find ways to connect with people. Some, like Mother Teresa, simply care so much for others that people are naturally drawn to them. The one thing they all have in common, though, is that they made people feel better about themselves just by being around.

In his book *Winning with People*, John Maxwell tells the story of a college psychology professor who required his students to pay a genuine compliment to three different people each day for one month. The students were upset with this assignment at first, but soon saw that over the course of those thirty days their relationships with people began to change. All-in-all, the students found that their behaviors toward others had a major impact on how those people acted toward them.

The professor was trying to teach his students that they could change the way people interacted with them by changing the way they interacted with those people. Basically, he was teaching them to be more charismatic. He also wanted them to know it was a skill they could learn. Charisma is like any other skill. It has fundamental components that can be understood, practiced, and improved. If you want to become a more charismatic leader, you just have to work on those fundamentals. If you do, charisma will just be a natural result.

The best way to enhance your charisma skills is to add a little SPICE to yourself. I believe there are five central charisma fundamentals that every leader can improve. Each of these traits make it much easier for others to want to be with you and want to be led by you. They are Self-confidence, Personality, Interest, Competence, and Empathy.

Charisma SPICE

Self-confidence: Before others will want to follow you, they must have confidence in your ability. It's easier for them to believe you know what you're doing when you believe you know what you're doing.

Personality: People have to know you and connect with you before they will want to be with you. Having a good personality will help them do both. Many folks believe you can't learn to improve your personality, but it is a skill you can develop. It's directly connected to the choice you make regarding your attitude. When you choose a good attitude you're automatically choosing a better personality. Even if you struggle with that choice, you can make big strides with your image just by smiling more often, laughing with others, and asking questions that lead to positive responses.

Interest: The number one way to make people feel good about the time they spend with you is to take an interest in them. If you spend more time talking about them than you spend talking about yourself, you will naturally draw others into any conversation.

Competence: Charismatic leaders are usually good conversationalists. The catch is you'll never be a good conversationalist if you can't add something to conversations. Anything you learn adds to your ability to connect with other people. Whether it's your profession, the arts, sports, or history, you put yourself in a better position to add value to conversations when you add value to yourself. Plus, people who value your opinion will also value your leadership. You can be foolish and charismatic and people may want to be around you, but you can't be foolish and charismatic and expect people to follow you.

Empathy: I believe the most important element in any human relationship is understanding. If you want to make others feel comfortable with you, they have to believe you have a good understanding of them and what they do. You just have to spend time with your teammates so you can better understand them; then make every effort to be understanding with them.

Tell your story.

People have to believe in you before they will follow you. You just have to give them a reason to believe. We can't expect that people will assume we are worth following because we hold a certain position and tell them what to do. Relationships are not built through positions and information. Annette Simmons, author of *The Story Factor*, once wrote, "People don't want more information. They are up to their eyeballs in information. They want faith – faith in you, in your goals, in your success, in your story."

Your story will let people know who you are and give them a chance to connect with you. It's that connection that will allow you to build the type of mutual understanding that will make it easier for your teammates to choose to follow you. As Ms. Simmons went on to say, "Other methods of influence – persuasion, bribery, or appeals – are push strategies. Story is a pull strategy. If your story is good enough, people – of their own free will – come to the conclusion they can trust you and the message you bring."

Quite Simply, Next-Level Relationships Are About...

...connections.

Your connection with your team will determine your effectiveness as a leader. I like using the term connection to discuss team relationships because I think it more accurately portrays the type of interaction it takes to truly collaborate and function as one unit. Jamie Collins, a scoutmaster in one of our local Boy Scout troops, once offered me a great explanation of the difference between a relationship and a connection. He told me, "You can have a relationship based on the fact that you share a space with someone. It doesn't mean you have a connection. That has to be personal." His point was that a relationship could exist based on people's proximity to one another. A connection only happens when you *feel* like you're together.

Leadership doesn't exist based on location. It can only exist based on a personal connection. If your teammates feel connected with you, you will have an opportunity to influence them. Take Paul Revere for example. Nearly every American knows of his midnight ride to warn people in the Boston area that "The British (were) coming!" We know his name because he successfully inspired others to action. Very few people, however, know that a man by the name of William Dawes showed the same courage by making the same ride that night. So why haven't we heard of him? Well, he wasn't as successful.

You see, Paul Revere had developed many personal relationships with the people. Dawes was an introvert and didn't have the same connections. The men and women of the Boston area didn't know him or why they should listen to him. Because of his lack of connection, Dawes didn't have the clout with the people to make the message meaningful.

For a team to be successful, the bonds have to extend beyond just those shared between the leader and follower, though. All teammates must feel connected. An old Welsh proverb reads, "He that would be a leader must be a bridge." You build that bridge by facilitating the same interactions amongst your teammates as you try to build for yourself. You have to give them a chance to strengthen their own relationships by giving them opportunities to get to know each other and each other's stories, too. If you teach your team how to see the world through the eyes of others and teach them the importance of making others feel good about themselves, you will do more than just improve their skills as leaders. You will improve their skills as teammates.

Leaders of groups must not only interact and communicate, but facilitate interaction and communication amongst the team. If you want to build a team, it starts with their desire to work together and support one another. In other words, it starts with their connections. Simply assigning people to do the same work or giving them the same goals doesn't make them a team. It makes them a group. A group is defined by its location. A team is defined by its connection.

Next-Level Self-Confidence

Confidence is contagious. So is lack of confidence.

Vince Lombardi

I think leadership is at its best when the leader is comfortable in that position. Part of being comfortable is being confident. Self-confidence is a feeling on the inside that affects our behaviors, so when you don't feel strong on the inside, it's hard to project strength on the outside. That strength makes a big difference in our ability to lead. Confident leaders have the courage to empower others, recognize accomplishments, listen to honest opinions, embrace change, accept accountability, try new things, set high standards, and surround themselves with great people. Think of the value a leader can add to a team by representing those principles.

A big part of that value is the power self-confidence has to unify others in one direction. There will be times when you will have to make a difficult decision, plan for the future, or initiate change. For any team to reach its potential during these times, everyone must be pulling in the same direction. If they don't have confidence in that direction, they're not going to go very far. If <u>you</u> don't have confidence in that direction, they may not even take the first step.

Professor and consultant Dr. Marshall Goldsmith advises, "There are never right or wrong answers to complex business decisions. The best you can do as a leader is to gather all of the information you can, do a cost-benefit analysis of potential options, use your best judgment, and then go for it." People are ultimately unified and inspired by you, not your decisions. They expect you to make those. That's your job. What they need is strength and stability afterwards. That's how they know everything is under control.

When it all comes down to it, your team wants you to be self-confident. No one wants to follow a timid or sheepish leader. They want to know that when you lead them down a path you believe it's the best one to take. They want to know that you are strong enough to have their back and give them the support they need to succeed. They want to know that you believe everyone is going to achieve their goals. If they don't believe these things, they'll question your decisions, doubt your ability, and hesitate to follow. Leaders must inspire confidence in others, but it's impossible if you have none in yourself. Simply put, you cannot give what you do not have.

Next Level: Instilling Confidence in Others

Everyone is afraid of something, and everyone has some aspect of his or her job that makes them a bit nervous. It's a natural feeling, but it's also a barrier to performance. Before anyone can achieve at high levels they must first believe they can achieve. Great leaders work to instill confidence in their followers because teams with little ability, but a lot of belief in that ability, are often more capable than teams with a lot of ability but little belief. As author Richard Bach once wrote, "sooner or later, those who win are those who think they can."

Those people are also the ones who continue to win because they are the people who believe they can improve. Conversely, a lack of self-confidence doesn't just keep people from using their talent; it keeps them from developing their talent. When people are unsure about doing something, they usually won't do it very well. At that point they might stop trying. That's when potential is limited.

Many people try to work on their self-confidence by practicing their eye contact or trying to stand up a little straighter in public, but those are just surface fixes. In order to become more self-confident, we have to change how we feel rather than just changing how we look. Self-confidence isn't about covering up fear. It's about removing it. The more fear you remove from your teammates, the further they will go.

To build a more confident team, you have to give your teammates chances to believe in themselves. Those chances don't always happen on their own. The team environment is sometimes a tough dynamic because at any moment any person can experience a barrier or a problem that has the potential to shut him or her down. If those individuals start to withdraw or decrease their performance as a result, the whole team weakens. We're only as strong as our weakest link, you know.

You build people's self-confidence by letting them experience success. Let them take control when the opportunity presents itself and let them be "right" as much as possible. Meetings, projects, decisions, and conversations are not contests. If you're always putting yourself in a position to be right, then you're always putting your team in a position to be wrong. If that becomes the norm, then all you're doing is creating a culture of losers.

One of the greatest things we can do to help support this kind of growth in our teammates is to put them in a place where they can play to their strengths, not their weaknesses. Most often, a lack of self-confidence is nothing more than a focus on the things we don't do well. If you want to give your teammates a boost, allow them to spend as much time as possible focusing on the things they're really good at doing.

Regardless of how you do it, though, your job is to add value to people's lives by increasing their ability. Leaders and coaches have to correct behavior, improve performance, and solve problems in order for the team to be successful. Those actions help the team perform at higher levels, but they can often feel intimidating or demeaning. It's how you address those areas that will determine how your teammates feel about themselves.

When you only focus on punishing bad behavior, it doesn't necessarily mean good behavior will take its place, and certainly does nothing to build people's belief in themselves. Teammates will be much more likely to embrace the positives if they realize the only reason for confrontation is a desire to make them better. As a result, they will be much more likely to use the feedback to build future confidence because of the increased skill than they will be to lose confidence because of what was said.

Where We Go Wrong

We are not prepared.

Preparation is the best self-confidence aid in the world. A lack of self-confidence is often nothing more than a lack of certainty. If you want to improve your confidence, improve your certainty. I don't care if you're delivering a speech, confronting a problem employee, making a decision, or entering the change-leadership process, when you put in the time to prepare yourself you will be much more confident doing what you have to do.

Preparation by its very definition means that you are getting ready for the future. It's much easier to feel confident about the future when you feel like you're prepared for it. That's why international entrepreneur Jim Rohn often teaches the Ant Philosophy when he counsels young leaders. One of his principles is that ants think "winter" all summer long in order to be confident they will survive the cold season. Of course, to do that they have to prepare during the warmer months. Because they do, they don't worry about the bad weather of the coming season. The same holds true for us. Quarterly goals aren't scary on the 90th day if we've spent the first 89 preparing.

We fear failure.

My first piece of advice to any leader struggling with his or her self-confidence is always, "Don't try to be perfect." It's an impossible expectation, and it leads us to adopt an unhealthy attitude toward failure. Problems will occur and bad decisions will be made. It doesn't mean you're doing a bad job. In fact, it's part of the job. When those things happen, it's your responsibility to get a handle on the situation and get going again.

Self-confidence should not be built on success alone. The truth is we learn a great deal from our failures. If we understand failure, we can embrace it as a means of improving our future skills, regardless of the temporary setback. Failing is not a permanent state unless we quit trying. We will all fail, but having a strong sense of self-confidence keeps us from being a failure. The difference is that failing allows you to learn and move forward. Failure means you quit moving, altogether.

With the courage to fail comes the courage to try. One of the best examples of this philosophy is the story of two rookie outfielders playing their first professional baseball game back in 1954. One played for the Cincinnati Reds and went 4 for 5 while helping his team win a one-run game. The other played for the Milwaukee Braves and went 0 for 5 in a losing effort. The winner's name was Jim Greengrass. The loser's name was Hank Aaron. If Mr. Aaron had viewed that experience as anything but an attempt from which he could learn, he would not have gone on to be Major League Baseball's homerun king.

We cross the line between confidence and arrogance.

Having the confidence to get better is a very constructive quality. Having the confidence that you are better than everyone else is a very destructive one. Having too much self-confidence can lead us to believe that our opinion is more important than someone else's or that our decisions are always the best. We should be confident in order to support people and unify direction, not compete with them and get our way.

Everyone wants to follow a confident hero. No one wants to follow an arrogant jerk. The problem is that it's often a very short distance between the two. To me, the line that separates self-confidence and arrogance is the Leadership Point-of-View. If what you do is driven by the best interests of others, you won't have to worry about the vanity associated with arrogance. I believe any leader should want to avoid arrogant behavior as a matter of principle, but it's also an important image to consider when trying to build influence with others. Confidence means your team will follow you up any mountain. Arrogance means they will want to knock you off of it!

How to Improve Your Self-Confidence

Embrace criticism, critique, and constructive feedback.

When you are in a leadership position, very few of the people with whom you work will have ever done your job, but everyone will have an opinion about how you should do it. If you're going to lead, you have to be okay with that critique. It's just something you have to accept. The only way to avoid criticism would be to avoid action. As Aristotle said, "Criticism is something you can avoid by saying nothing, doing nothing, and being nothing." Your team needs much more than that from their leader.

Actually, criticism and critique are very valuable. They're really just forms of feedback. After many years of working to become a better leader I have come to realize that it's not the advice you give that will determine your success; it's the advice you take. All good leaders know how to give criticism as a means of improving the performance of their teammates. The great ones know how to take it as a means of improving their own. We've spoken of the importance of knowing how to positively *give* constructive feedback, but you can only improve your ability if you positively *take* it. Below are a few tips for using criticism to your full advantage.

Tips for Taking Constructive Feedback

Listen without emotion. We get defensive when others critique our performance because of feelings, not information. If you focus on the information you may just find a piece of feedback that allows you to make life-altering improvements.

Understand criticism. Criticism is really just a type of insight, and insight is a very valuable gift. When people give you feedback, they are basically giving you the chance to get better. When you look back over your life you will most likely find that the people who truly cared for you were the ones who told you what you needed to hear.

Turn destructive criticism into constructive criticism. Take the approach that anything negative you hear about your performance is a chance to eliminate bad behavior. If you can take anything away from someone's negative comments that allows you to improve, you should be thankful for the opportunity.

Know that you're not alone. Every leader will be scrutinized at some point. Dr. Martin Luther King, Jr. was one of the greatest leaders the world has ever known, yet he was also one of the most criticized. If he had focused on the negativity, he would not have been so likely to serve as such a positive example for millions of people.

Draw strength from others.

Overcoming the fear associated with a lack of confidence can be tough, so many times we need someone to help. I've been very fortunate to have many people throughout my life do just that. Usually they did it by giving me the structure and support I needed to overcome my fears. Many of the self-confidence skills I have developed as a leader were the result of those efforts.

For instance, one of my strengths is public speaking. People will often tell me, "I wish I were as comfortable as you talking to a crowd of people. It just comes so natural for you." I tell them I appreciate the compliment, but it was anything but natural. I used to be terrified of crowds. Folks who know me now are very surprised to hear that I dropped out of my basic public speaking course in college. Twice! The first time I dropped the course we had to give a one-minute speech on the first day about who we were and why we were going to college. I asked to be excused so I could run to the restroom before we got started, and never went back.

I ended up taking the course two years later because I needed it to graduate. I forced myself to give that first speech, but afterwards decided that I would change my major to anything that didn't require me to take that class. My instructor, Dr. Rebecca Pettys, must have sensed my fear. She pulled me aside after class and said, "Juston, you have one of the strongest voices I've ever heard and you tell stories better than any college student I've ever met. You just have to get up on stage and share your talents with people."

From that day forward, I decided to give it my best shot, and Dr. Pettys gave me the encouragement and constructive feedback I needed to get me through the tough spots. She praised me when I needed it and corrected me when I made mistakes. She criticized me enough to improve my skills and praised me enough to make me believe in them. She made me feel so good about being in front of people that I ended up acting in several college plays. Now, because of her investment in my confidence, my life is not limited by a fear of public speaking.

Remember why you do what you do.

Sometimes it's really hard to confront the issues you must address as a leader. Those difficult times can really shake your confidence and bring out some really anxious feelings. Usually it feels that way because we focus on the difficulty of the task, not the necessity of the action. If you change your focus a bit to let the "why" you have to do something drive your actions rather than the "how" you have to do it, you will have a much easier time getting over the fear of the confrontation.

For example, I have had to conduct a few meetings with high school and college instructors over the years who were not doing a good job teaching their students. Now, that's a really tough conversation to have with highly dedicated people who love what they do and care about their students. Still, there are times when it comes to my attention that someone (for whatever reason) just isn't performing well in the classroom.

I have been criticized and cussed for even approaching the subject, but the hard truth is that if I allow the poor performance to continue, the students are the ones who suffer. By keeping them in mind, I don't feel nearly as reserved about initiating that conversation. Plus, because I care about the people with whom I work, I want them to do the best job they can do. I want them to be remembered as a positive influence on other people's lives, not a burden. If I never let those teammates know when they are not performing well, how can they ever improve?

Surround yourself with confident people.

Coach Vince Lombardi once said that confidence is contagious. It's true, and it applies to everyone on the team. You always want to be a source of confidence for your teammates, but there's nothing wrong with letting them do the same for you. I can't tell you how much confidence it gives me to know that when times are hard, I have such a strong team surrounding me. Their strength becomes my strength, and I know that together there's nothing we can't overcome.

Steve Jobs, the founder of Apple Computers, knew this principle well. In fact, he built his company on it. People have called him an entrepreneur, a visionary, an innovator, and a genius. Of all of his leadership qualities, though, the true secret to his success may have been his self-confidence. He surrounded himself with the best people he could find and gave them the freedom to do great things. He wasn't worried about his status within the company, even if he hired someone who was considered to be the best in their field.

To market his Apple product, he hired Regis McKenna, who was known as the best marketing executive in the business. Jobs knew when he hired him that McKenna would probably have better ideas about marketing, but he wanted the best ideas, not the credit. Even more impressive, Jobs knew his strengths were not managerial so he decided he needed to hire someone with business experience to run his company. He hired John Sculley, the highly successful CEO of Pepsi, to be the new CEO of Apple. Talk about a move that required confidence! Every time he added a great individual to his team, though, it gave him more confidence that he was going to accomplish his goals. It's the combination of that confidence and that team that has led Apple to be one of the most profitable companies in the world.

At Its Most Basic Level, Next-Level Self-Confidence Is...

...freedom.

Self-confidence is much more than just an important element to success. It's also a really good feeling. Nothing beats the freedom that self-confidence brings. It helps you overcome paranoia, doubt, and insecurity. It allows you surround yourself with great people, listen to their opinions, set high expectations, and accept accountability. It also means that you are free to admit your mistakes so you never have to hide behind them and are free to ask for help any time you think you might need it.

Perhaps just as important, self-confidence gives everyone the freedom to have a positive outlook. Freedom from fear is another way of saying freedom from negativity. Negative attitudes often creep in as a result of some type of fear about our performance or our future. Either of those has the potential to bring us down if we don't believe in ourselves enough to feel as though we're going to end up in a better place.

It's a concept that's even more important to our effect on others. It's hard to convince someone that you're leading them to a better place if you don't feel positive about your own direction. It's much easier to have a positive effect on others and inspire them to believe in themselves if you maintain a healthy outlook and feel good about yourself.

Above all else, a strong sense of self-confidence means that you are free to try. People who don't believe in themselves or their abilities let the fear of failure limit their lives and become much less likely to set lofty goals for themselves. It's not really the failure those people fear, though. It's the accountability for the failure.

The first step in accomplishing any goal is having the guts to commit to it. Of course, once you commit to something, you become accountable for the results. Success comes much easier when you don't fear the accountability that comes from that commitment. While your work ethic and perseverance truly determine how likely you will be to reach your goals, it's the confidence to commit to those goals that will give you a chance in the first place.

Next-Level Influence

The key to successful leadership today is influence, not authority.

Kenneth Blanchard

P eople who are successful in business, medicine, administration, or any other field aren't successful because of the job they have; they're successful because of the job they do. It's the person, not the position that matters. I think Bear Bryant would have been a great military man, just as I believe Gen. Colin Powell would have been a great football coach. I believe Father Theodore Hesburgh would have made a fine business leader, just as I believe Jack Welch would have made a fine college president. I believe Pat Summitt would have been a strong politician, and I believe Margaret Thatcher would have been a championship basketball coach.

Those individuals were not successful because of *what* they were. They were successful because of *who* they were and what they meant to the people they led. It wasn't necessarily because they knew more or could do more than anyone else; it was because they had the ability to get more out of everyone else. Leadership isn't a title. It's a quality found in people, not positions. That quality is not called coach, general, Prime Minister, or CEO. That quality is called influence.

The three phases of leadership (Choosing Direction, Aligning Work with Goals, and Building Influence) are all essential, but it would be easy to argue that building influence is the most important. Having influence means that you are important enough to someone to change their direction. The work we do as leaders to build trust, respect, and a connection with our team is done so that we may become important enough to them to make a difference in their lives.

The decisions and plans we make set the boundaries for what the team will do, but it's the work your team does and the decisions they make that actually get the results. How well their decisions and actions align with what you need them to do will depend on the amount of influence you have built with them. It's their commitment to you that will determine their commitment to your direction. I believe there are three levels of follower commitment to the leader: Pulling Teeth, Pulling Their Weight, and Pulling for You. Into which category your teammates fall will determine the level to which you will rise.

Pulling Teeth – Your team follows because they feel like they have to. In this case they will most likely do what you say, but may not give it all they've got.

Pulling Their Weight – Your team follows because it's the right thing to do. The problem is that everyone may also do the work *they* feel is the right thing to do, not necessarily the work that will unify the team in one direction.

Pulling for You – Your team follows because they want to. When people want to follow your lead, they will want your decisions to succeed. In this case, you will not only get them working in the right direction, but you will get their best effort along the way.

Regardless of the level of influence we have with other people, our goal should be to use it to add value to their lives. The great thing about using your influence to add value to others is that it's also the best way to build more influence. If the influence you've built with your teammates adds value to their lives, they will be capable of doing more. When they become more capable, they will experience more success, which in turn builds your influence with them. The more influence you have with them, the more you can inspire additional growth. I call this the Circle of Influence.

Circle of Influence

Circle diagram:

Influence → Allows you to.. → **Add Value to Others** → Because of this, your teammates... → **Increase Their Ability** → Which leads them to find more... → **Success** → Which means you gain... → **Influence**

I do believe it when I say that leadership is not about you; it's about your effect. That effect will be measured by the impact you have made on the lives of your teammates. That impact can only be felt through the power of influence.

Next Level: Image Projection

Influence has nothing to do with how you feel, what you think, or the quality of your intentions. Those are feelings inside of you. What truly matters is how others feel about you, care about what you think, or believe about your intentions. For instance, to gain influence with others, it's not enough to be honest, caring, and ethical. For you to gain influence with your teammates, they have to *know* you're honest, *believe* you care, and *share* your values.

Leadership only exists when there are followers. For this reason, their opinion of you is very important. If they don't see you as a leader worth following, they may not follow, at all. The image you project is how others perceive you, and perception is most certainly reality. If the team doesn't see you as the leader, you can't lead them. If you want to build your influence, strive to project the following images:

Consistent – Before you can have influence with anyone, they have to feel comfortable letting you into their lives. People will keep their distance if they don't know whether you're going to pat on their back or bite off their head.

Ethical – Being ethical is more than just knowing what's right. It's doing what's right. If people believe you will do the right things, they'll have an easier time believing you will do the right things for them.

Hardworking – If your team believes you are lazy or disinterested, no amount of motivation, memos, or mandates will inspire them to work hard for you.

Honest – People will never believe in your direction if they can't believe in you.

Intelligent – I'll just put this bluntly: nobody wants to follow a fool. If you want to make it easy for others to follow you, they can't perceive you as goofy, silly, or incompetent.

Kind – Courtesy and kindness are people attractors. Influence is a connection, and it's easier to connect with someone you know will treat you well.

Open-Minded – Leaders with the most influence are willing to be influenced, themselves. When your teammates know you are willing to seek new and better ways, it's easier for them to believe the path you choose is the right one.

Positive – I don't know about you, but I want to follow someone who believes we have a brighter future. Otherwise, I really don't want to go where they're going.

Strong – People want to know their leader can handle the job. If you freak out at the first sign of trouble, your team will look for leadership elsewhere when times get tough.

Well-Spoken – Naomi Judd's mother once told her, "Words are like the clothes you wear, and I want you to be well-dressed." What you say represents what you think, but how you say it represents who you are. Both will affect the amount of influence you gain with your team.

If your goal is to make a difference in people's lives, you'll want to make it as easy as possible for them to get on board with you and what you're doing. Image has a profound effect on how willing others will be to follow you. You have to be a quality leader before you can positively impact people's lives, but they have to believe you're a quality leader before they will let you.

Where We Go Wrong

We lack intention.

Some folks believe that influence and leadership are the same thing, but I think there is one key difference. If left all to itself, influence can happen whether it was intended or not. Leadership must be intentional. For instance, if I see George Clooney wear a shirt I like, I might be influenced to buy that shirt. If you overhear someone talking about a great movie, their conversation may influence you to go see it this weekend. Those are examples of influence, but not the *intentional* influence that translates to leadership.

Influence must be both intentionally built and intentionally used. Leaders who leave influence up to chance may improve the lives of others, but only if the followers are looking to grow. Strong leaders seek opportunities to initiate and guide that growth. That type of leadership takes more time and energy than the work it takes to manage processes, but if you want to make a difference, it's well worth the effort.

We confuse power and influence.

Many leaders seek power instead of influence, or they mistakenly rely on power to try to build their influence. The problem is that while power and influence are related, they are two different things. The difference becomes apparent when you look at the reasons followers respond to a leader. Power leaders *make* people do what they do. Influence leaders *inspire* people to do what they do. You can't build a following by making people do things. You build a following by becoming important to them and adding value to their lives as a result.

Power does have a place in leadership, though. It brings a certain sense of credibility and confidence to the position. Those are very admirable qualities when looking to someone for guidance. Authors Bob Briner and Ray Pritchard agree and believe that the best leaders teach with authority. Before reading their book I had never thought about it like that before, but the best teachers and leaders I've ever had taught with a certainty that just made me believe in them. I didn't doubt them, so their message had more influence with me.

Leaders who deny their power or seem uncomfortable with it actually lose influence with their team because they are viewed as weak or ill-suited for the job. To make the best use of power, you just have to keep a few rules in mind.

Be humble. Using power to build yourself up only tears you down.

Wield it sparingly. You're supposed to lead people, not drive them.

To gain it, give it away. The power you give to others comes back tenfold.

Don't apologize for it. It's yours and can be used to strengthen the team.

Don't force it. If you have to prove it, you probably don't have it.

Just remember that influence is always a much better motivator than power. Power leaders rely on status or intimidation to motivate performance, which may be effective in the short-term but harmful in the long-term. Think about it this way: who is more powerful? The boss who gets something done because she said to do it, or the boss who gets something done because others wanted to do it for her? With power, people follow an order. With influence, people follow a leader.

We seek the wrong level of respect.

Many leaders get into trouble because they don't understand that leadership respect is different than interpersonal respect. People may show each other a good deal of common courtesy and earn social respect, but for a team to respect a leader it takes much, much more. Respect plays a very important role in any healthy relationship, but you need to know what level you must earn to develop strong leader/follower relationships.

To be effective in a position of authority, you must have earned respect as a person, a peer, and an advisor. The following pyramid represents those varying degrees of respect and their relationship to the people who choose to follow you. At each tier, the pyramid contains the elements of leadership that must exist before you can earn that particular level of respect.

Pyramid of Respect

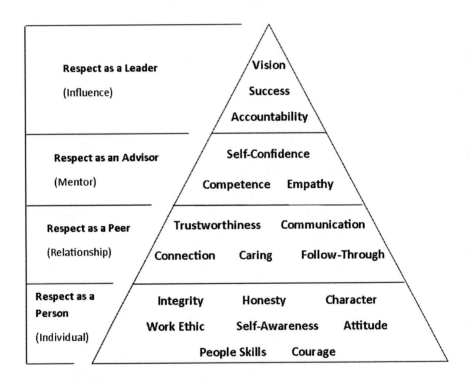

Like Maslow's famous *Hierarchy of Needs*, each level builds on the one below it. For example, you can't reach the third tier without building the elements in the first two tiers. It's impossible to be respected as an Advisor if you aren't respected as a Person or a Peer. It takes time and effort to be respected as a leader, but it's the only way to earn influence with your teammates.

How to Gain More Influence with Others

Add value to people's lives.

When it all comes down to it, the most important thing any leader can do is improve the lives of those who choose to follow them. It's the only way to build a successful team. Organizations don't provide services, and they don't produce products. People provide services and produce products. Leaders who develop great people are the ones who ultimately make a difference. One leader who valued that principle was one of the earliest African American leaders in American history, Bishop Daniel Payne.

Bishop Payne used the power of influence to make a difference in the lives of thousands during his life, and many more since his passing in 1891. He was born during the slavery era of American history, but he was born free and lived his life as a free man. He wasn't satisfied to keep his good fortune to himself, though. He wanted to use his status as a platform to help other African Americans. Since he had the freedom to become educated, he made it his life's mission to add value to his life for the sole purpose of adding value to others.

Payne found his calling in the African Methodist Episcopal (AME) Church. He quickly gained significant influence within the organization and used his newly acquired position of bishop to move the AME church into the South after the Civil War. He was not satisfied to just build churches, however. He wanted to build people and leaders. He went on to found a college for African American students called Wilberforce University, where he served as the first black president of an American college.

Bishop Payne made himself valuable for the sole purpose of returning that value to others. Because of this, his influence spread far and wide. Today, the AME Church has congregations all over the world with more than two million members and Wilberforce is still a thriving institution, enrolling nearly 850 students each year.

Personally, I was taught to start thinking about the influence we have on people's lives at a very young age. As a boy I remember my pastor, Bob Landis, telling us that it's our job to pour goodness into others. That philosophy stuck with me. Ever since, I have tried to constantly be aware of what I'm pouring into other people. If I do nothing more than pour goodness into the people around me over the course of my life and career, I believe I will have done my job. In fact, I'm not sure there's a more important job that I could do.

Set high expectations.

Influence is only worthwhile if we use it to make a positive difference. People will very often rise to high expectations. Just be aware that they will very often rise to low expectations, as well. When you set low expectations for others, your impact on their lives is insignificant. The only way to inspire them to greatness is to expect greatness from them.

One of my favorite stories about setting and communicating high expectations occurred during Coach Lou Holtz's first season at Notre Dame. Holtz had inherited a decent football team with good athletes and a solid quarterback named Steve Berlein. There was a problem, though. Berlein threw too many interceptions for the team to win many games. When Coach Holtz reviewed the films from the previous season it was clear that if Berlein had thrown fewer interceptions, Notre Dame would have won more games.

When Holtz met with his young quarterback, he said, "Steve, I guarantee that you will not throw more than six interceptions this season." Berlein was elated, and asked Holtz if he had a special offensive scheme that would keep him from throwing the ball to the other team. Coach Holtz said, "No. You won't throw seven interceptions because when you throw the sixth one you're sitting on the bench for the rest of the season."

The expectations had been clearly set, and Berlein responded with a stellar season. It was the first time in his career that he had thrown more touchdowns than interceptions. Berlein went on to a 17-year NFL career, where he threw 147 touchdowns and amassed almost 25,000 yards. The turnaround was not due to a change in his throwing style or a new type of offensive scheme. The only thing that changed was the expectations of his leader.

Lead your life to lead the lives of others.

People who simply live their lives are the ones who respond to whatever circumstances the world creates for them. They usually rely on the guidance of others to make their way. People who *lead* their lives are the ones who create their own successes. They are proactive with the world and make their circumstances work out for the best. Those are the people who gain influence with me because I believe they're heading to a better place, and I'd like to go with them.

This is the reason that over 300 slaves followed Harriet Tubman to freedom during the pre–Civil War era in the United States. They didn't follow her because of a title, her status, or an executive order. She had none of those things. They followed her because she found a way to make a better life for herself, and they believed she could help them do the same.

She led her life and changed her circumstances, ultimately putting her in a position to change many others. With each of the successful 19 missions she led on the Underground Railroad, she gained more influence because she proved she could make a difference. Her accomplishments also earned her a good deal of influence with prominent politicians and civil leaders (both white and black) after the Civil War. Even William Seward, the U. S. Secretary of State, sought her counsel. This influence was earned because she didn't rely on others for her outcomes. She led her life, which gave her the capacity to lead others.

When All Is Said and Done, Next-Level Influence Is...

...your legacy.

When we have moved on, we will leave behind three things: some stuff, some work, and some people. Throughout your life, you will have made investments of time and energy in each. You'll have to choose which of the three are most important to you. Just remember that the stuff will be passed around from person to person and the work will be forgotten once the next initiative begins. The people, however, will live on.

I heard a woman speak at a seminar a few years back who said there are basically three phases in life. First, you learn. You experience all that you can in an effort to grow yourself and make yourself more valuable to the world. Then, you earn. You reap the rewards for the time you spent adding value to yourself. Finally, you return. It's in this stage of life you return the knowledge and wealth you collected to others so that when your life ends, your impact lives on. Without returning, all the value you've gained ends with you.

Returning value to others is a wonderful philosophy, and it's the best approach to leadership I know. Investments in people are really the ones that make a difference. Leaders who don't believe in this principle hold their organizations back because they hold their people back. I once overheard a conversation between two CEOs that pretty much summed up the importance of this concept. The first CEO asked, "What if I train my employees and they leave? The money I invested in their education would be wasted." To which the second CEO responded, "What if you don't train them and they stay?"

It's the investments we make in others that truly determine our legacy as leaders. Amos Alonzo Stagg, the great University of Chicago football coach from the early 1900s, was once congratulated on a successful season by a reporter who yelled, "It was a great year, coach!" To which Coach Stagg replied, "We won't know that for another twenty years or so." Stagg knew that the impact of our influence isn't realized in a moment. It's not even realized in our lifetime. It's realized in the lives and lifetimes of others.

For example, while Attila the Hun built one of the most formidable forces in human history, the Hun nation fell apart soon after his death. During his reign, he didn't return any of the value that had been added to his life by investing it in the future of his people. Because of this, no one could carry on his legacy. Mother Teresa, on the other hand, dedicated her entire life to adding value to the lives of others. She founded a small humanitarian group called The Sisters of

Loreto. When Mother Teresa died, she left such a powerful legacy that the organization has grown to 4,000 nuns and over 120,000 lay workers around the world.

Success in work leads to some thrilling moments; success in life follows you throughout all of your days, but success in others lasts long after you're gone. When all is said and done, I don't think I could say it any better than one of my former students. A young woman by the name of Misty Sergent once wrote in a short essay, "I believe that life and life works are not measurable. I believe they are only memorable. You will be remembered for what you did for others."

All the things we do to choose the right direction for our followers, align their work with their goals, and build influence is done so that we may have a positive impact on their lives. I will close this chapter and this book with one final thought, and one parting question. When we are gone, we don't leave behind a reputation, a set of things, or a memory; we leave behind the next generation. What are you going to do to make sure it's a good one?

Notes

Introduction

Bennis W. & Nanus, B. (1997). *Leaders: The Strategies for Taking Charge.* HarperCollins Publishers: New York.

Maxwell, J. C. (2007). *21 Irrefutable Laws of Leadership: Follow Them and People Will Follow You.* Thomas Nelson: Nashville.

Riggio, R. E. (2008). Leadership Development: The Current State and Future Expectations. *Consulting Psychology Journal: Practice and Research, 60*(4), 383-392.

Smith, S. A. (2013). *Marriage Isn't For You.* Retrieved November 4, 2013 from http://sethadamsmith.com/2013/11/02/marriage-isnt-for-you/).

Section I – Choosing Direction

Next-Level Integrity

Baldoni, J. (2003). *Great Communication Secrets of Great Leaders.* McGraw-Hill: New York.

Bass, B., & Bass, R. (2008). *The Bass Handbook of Leadership: Theory, Research, & Managerial Applications* (4th ed.) Free Press: New York.

Benner, R. B. (2007). Virtue Theory and Leadership Theory: Cross-Cultural Models for Administrators and Faculty, in Hellmich, D. M. (2007). *Ethical Leadership in the Community College: Bridging Theory and Daily Practice.* Anker Publishing Compnay: Bolton, MA.

Boisjoly, R. P., Curtis, E. F., & Mellican, E. (1989). Roger Boisjoly and the Challenger Disaster: The Ethical Dimensions. *Journal of Business Ethics. 8,* 4, 217-230.

Hellmich, D. M. (2007). *Ethical Leadership in the Community College: Bridging Theory and Daily Practice.* Anker Publishing Compnay: Bolton, MA.

Henriques, D. B., (2012). *The Wizard of Lies: Bernie Madoff and the Death of Trust.* St. Martin's Griffin: New York.

Kent, K. (1968). *The Paradoxical Commandments.* Excerpt from: *The Silent Revolution: Dynamic Leadership in the Student Council.* Retrieved February 5, 2014 from http://www.paradoxicalcommandments.com/origin.html.

Machiavelli, N. (1995). *The Prince,* translated by David Wootton. Hackett Publishing: Indianapolis.

Thomas, A. B. (1988). Does Leadership Make a Difference to Organizational Performance? *Administrative Science Quarterly, 33,* 388-400.

Vagelos, R. & Galambos, L. (2006). *The Moral Corporation: Merck Experiences.* Cambridge University Press: Cambridge.

Next-Level Awareness

Baldoni, J. (2003). *Great Communication Secrets of Great Leaders.* McGraw-Hill: New York.

Biography.com Editors. (2014). George Custer. Retrieved November 26, 2014 from http://www.biography.com/people/george-custer-9264128.

Campbell, A., Whitehead, J., & Finkelstein, S. (2009). Why Good Leaders Make Bad Decisions. *Harvard Business Review.* Retrieved November 17, 2013 from http://hbr.org/2009/02/why-good-leaders-make-bad- decisions/.

Clawson, J. G. (2012). *Level Three Leadership: Getting Below the Surface* (5th Ed.). Prentice Hall: Boston.

Ericsson, K. A., Prietula, M. J., & Cokely, E. T. (2007). The Making of an Expert. *Harvard Business Review.* Jul–Aug, *85*(7-8), 114-121.

Goleman, D. (1995). *Emotional Intelligence.* Bantam: New York.

PBS.org. (2015). Depression and War: Down and Out. Retrieved March 15, 2015 from http://www.pbs.org/wnet/historyofus/web12/segment2.html.

Reed, M. (2013). *Confessions of a Community College Administrator.* Jossey-Bass: San Francisco.

Next-Level Philosophy

Michelli, J. A. (2007). *The Starbucks Experience: 5 Principles for Turning ordinary into Extraordinary.* McGraw-Hill: New York.

Rand, A. (1984). *Philosophy: Who needs it?* Signet: New York.

Next-Level Planning

Gates, B. (2007). Commencement Speech, Harvard. Retrieved January 11, 2014 from
http://www.youtube.com/watch?v=iADTpgRXYrk).

Maxwell, J. C. (2001). *Developing the Leader within You Workbook.* Thomas Nelson: Nashville.

Shakespeare, W. *Hamlet*, I.v.174-175 in Cohen, W., Howard, Je. E., Maus, K., E., & Greenblatt, S. (ed.). (1997). *The Norton Shakespeare.* W. W. Norton & Company: New York.

Sheehan, J. K. (2009). *A Leader Becomes a Leader: Inspirational Stories of Leadership for a New Generation.* True Gifts Publishing: Belmont, MA.

Womack, J., P. & Jones, D., T. (2003). *Lean Thinking: Banish Waste and Create Wealth in Your Corporation.* Simon and Schuster: New York.

Next-Level Decision-Making

Harvey, E., & Lucia, A. (2000). *144 Ways to Walk the Talk.* Performance Publishing Company: Dallas.

Kahneman, D. (2011). *Thinking Fast and Slow.* Farrar, Straus and Giroux: New York.

Polelle, M. R. (2008). *Leadership: Fifty Great Leaders and the Worlds They Made.* Greenwood Press: Westport, CT.

Rees, J. C. & Spignesi, S. (2007) *George Washington's Leadership Lessons: What the Father of Our Country Can Teach Us about Leadership and Character.* John Wiley & Sons: Hoboken.

Sample, S. B. (2002). *The Contrarian's Guide to Leadership.* San Francisco: Jossey-Bass.

Section II – Aligning Work with Success

Next-Level Alignment

Hughes, R. L., Ginnet, R. C., & Curphy, G, J. (2012). *Leadership: Enhancing the Lessons of Experience.* McGraw-Hill: New York.

Labovitz, G. & Rosansky, V. (1997). The Power of Alignment: How Great Companies Stay Centered and Accomplish Extraordinary Things. John Wiley and Sons, Inc.: New York.

Shobel, D. (1995). *Longitude.* Walker: New York.

Next-Level Communication

Biography.com Editors. (2014). Julius Robert Oppenheimer. Retrieved Nov 12, 2014 from http://www.biography.com/people/j-robert-oppenheimer-9429168.

Davis, K., Christodoulou, J., Seider, S., & Gardner, H. *The theory of Multiple Intelligences.* Retrieved Dec. 25, 2013 from http://howardgardner01.files.wordpress.com/2012/06/443-davis-christodoulou-seider-mi- article.pdf.

Harvey, E., & Lucia, A. (2000). *144 Ways to Walk the Talk*. Performance Publishing Company: Dallas.

Kelly, C. C., (2007). *The Manhattan Project: The Birth of the Atomic Bomb in the Words of Its Creators, Eyewitnesses, and Historians*. Black Dog & Leventhal Publishers, Inc.: New York.

Pitino, R. & Reynolds, B. (2000). *Lead to Succeed: 10 Traits of Great Leadership in Business and Life*. Broadway Books: New York.

Rabinowitz, B. (2013). Ohio State Football: Leaderhsip Class Even Has Meyer Taking Notes. *The Columbus Dispatch*. Retrieved November 12, 2013 from http://buckeyextra.dispatch.com/content/stories/2013/07/26/ leadership-class-even-has-meyer-taking-notes.html.

Next-Level Change-Leadership

CNBC.com. (2014). CNBC Profiles: Anne Mulcahy. Retrieved September 12, 2014 from http://www.cnbc.com/id/37596940/.

George, B. (2008). America's Best Leaders: Anne Mulcahy, Xerox CEO. *U.S. News & World Report*. Retrieved September 12, 2014 from http://www.usnews.com/news/best-leaders/articles/2008/11/19/americas- best-leaders-anne-mulcahy-xerox-ceo?page=2.

Maxwell, J. C. (2002). *The 21 Irrefutable Laws of Leadership Workbook*. Thomas Nelson: Nashville.

Utterback, J. M. (1994). *Mastering the Dynamics of Innovation*. Harvard Business School Press: Boston.

Next-Level Implementation

Abrashoff, B. M. (2004). *Get Your Ship Together: How Great Leaders Inspire Ownership from the Keel Up*. Penguin Books: New York.

Bayles, D. & Orland, T. (1993). Art and Fear: Observations on the Perils (And Rewards) of Artmaking. Capra Press: Santa Barbara.

Hughes, R. L., Ginnet, R. C., & Curphy, G, J. (2012). *Leadership: Enhancing the Lessons of Experience.* McGraw-Hill: New York.

USHistory.org. (2014). *The Declaration of Independence.* Retrieved November 1, 2014 from http://www.ushistory.org/Declaration/document/.

Next-Level Accountability

Anderson, C. R. (1977). Locus of Control, Coping Behaviors, and Performance in a Stress Setting: A Longitudinal Study. *Journal of Applied Psychology, 62,* 690-698.

Anderson, C. R., Hellriegel, D. & Slocum, J. W. (1977). Managerial Response to Environmentally Induced Stress. *Academy of Management Journal, 20,* 260-272.

Anderson, M. (2011). *212⁰ Leadership: 10 Rules for Highly Effective Leadership.* Simple Truths, LLC: Naperville, Il.

Blanchard, K. (2012). *The Heart of a Leader: Insights on the Art of Influence.* Simple Truths, LLC: Naperville, Il.

Carey, M. R. (1992). Transformational Leadership and the Fundamental Option for Self-Transcendence. *Leadership Quarterly, 3,* 217-236.

Durand, D. E. & Shea, D. (1974). Entrepreneurial Activity as a Function of Achievement Motivation and Reinforcement Control. *Journal of Psychology, 88,* 57-63.

Johnson, A. L., Luthans, F., & Hennessey, H. W. (1984). The Role of Locus of Control in Leader Influence Behavior. *Personnel Psychology, 37,* 61-75.

Rees, J. C. & Spignesi, S. (2007) *George Washington's Leadership Lessons: What the Father of Our Country Can Teach Us about Leadership and Character.* John Wiley & Sons: Hoboken.

Riesman, D., Glazer, N., & Denney, R. (2001). *The Lonely Crowd.*
Yale Nota Bene: New Haven.

Rubel, S. (2014). *Growing Up.* Retrieved Feb. 17, 2014 from
http://www.inspirationalstories.com /9/976.html.

Section III – Influencing Others to Follow

Next-Level Attitude

Baldoni, J. (2003). *Great Communication Secrets of Great Leaders.*
McGraw-Hill: New York.

Baxter, J. S. (1996). *Awake, My Heart.* Kregal Publicatoins: Grand
Rapids.

Brown, S. (2009). *Play: How it Shapes the Brain, Opens the Imagination,
and Invigorates the Soul.* Penguin Group: New York.

Center for Disease Control and Prevention. (2004). *Worker Health
Chartbook, 2004.* DHHS (NIOSH) Publication No. 2004–146.
Retrieved February 20, 2014 from
http://www.cdc.gov/niosh/docs/2004-146/pdfs/2004-
146.pdf.

Hughes, R. L., Ginnet, R. C., & Curphy, G, J. (2012). *Leadership:
Enhancing the Lessons of Experience.* McGraw-Hill: New York.

Mandela, N. (1994). *Long Walk to Freedom: The Autobiography of Nelson
Mandela.* Little, Brown and Company: New York.

McGregor, D. (1966) *Leadership and Motivation.* MIT Press: Cambridge.

Sheehan, J. K. (2009). *A Leader Becomes a Leader: Inspirational Stories of
Leadership for a New Generation.* True Gifts Publishing: Belmont,
MA.

Wooden, J. & Jamison, S. (1997). *Wooden: A Lifetime of Observations on
and off the Court.* McGraw-Hill: New York.

Next-Level Trust

Kouzes, J. M., & Posner, B. Z. (1996). *The Credibility Factor.* Jossey-Bass: San Francisco.

Maxwell, J. C. (2002). *The 21 Irrefutable Laws of Leadership Workbook.* Thomas Nelson: Nashville.

Peterson, D. B. & Hicks, M. D. (1996). *Leader as Coach: Strategies for Coaching and Developing Others.* Personal Decisions International: Minneapolis.

Petersen, D. E., & Hillkirk, J. (1991). *A Better Idea: Redefining the Way Americans Work.* Houghton Mifflin, Co.: Boston.

Next-Level Relationships

Hughes, R. L., Ginnet, R. C., & Curphy, G, J. (2012). *Leadership: Enhancing the Lessons of Experience.* McGraw-Hill: New York.

Maxwell, J. C. (2004). *Winning with People.* Thomas Nelson: Nashville.

Simmons, A. (2006). *The Story Factor: Inspiration, Influence, and Persuasion Through the Art of Storytelling.* Basic Books: New York.

Summitt, P. & Jenkins, S. (2013). *Sum it Up: 1,098 Victories, a Couple of Irrelevant Losses, and a Life in Perspective.* Crown Archetype: New York.

Next-Level Self-Confidence

Biography.com Editors. (2014). Attila the Hun. Retrieved July 23, 2014, from http://www.biography.com/people/attila-the-hun-9191831.

Goldsmith, M. (2007). *What Got You Here Won't Get You There: How Successful People Become Even More Successful.* Hyperion: New York.

Isaacson, W. (2011). *Steve Jobs.* Simon & Schuster: New York.

Maxwell, J. C. (2003). Attitude 101: What Every Leader Needs to Know. Thomas Nelson Publishers: Nashville.

Roberts, W. (2009). *Leadership Secrets of Attila the Hun*. Business Plus Hachette Book Group: New York.

Next-Level Influence

Bishop, R. S. (2009). *Bishop Daniel A. Payne: Great Black Leader*. Just Us Books: East Orange, NJ.

Briner, B. & Pritchard, R. (2008). *The Leadership Lessons of Jesus: A Timeless Model for Today's Leaders*. B & H Publishing Group: Nashville.

ESPN.com. (2014). Player Statistics. Retrieved October 20, 2014 from http://espn.go.com/nfl/player/stats/_/id/18/steve-beuerlein.

Holtz, L. (2006). Wins, Losses, and Lessons: An Autobiography. HarperCollins Publisher: New York.

Maxwell, J. C. (2002). *The 21 Irrefutable Laws of Leadership Workbook*. Thomas Nelson: Nashville.

Roberts, W. (2009). *Leadership Secrets of Attila the Hun*. Business Plus Hachette Book Group: New York.

Sterling, D. (1954). Freedom Train: The Story of Harriet Tubman. Scholastic, Inc.: New York.

CPSIA information can be obtained
at www.ICGtesting.com
Printed in the USA
FFOW02n1833180916
27638FF